Portraits from Life
by
Edmund Gosse

Portraits from Life
by
Edmund Gosse

edited with an introduction by

ANN THWAITE

Scolar Press

Published by
SCOLAR PRESS
Gower House
Croft Road
Aldershot
Hants GU11 3HR
England

Gower Publishing Company
Old Post Road
Brookfield
Vermont 05036
USA

British Library Cataloguing in Publication Data
Gosse, Edmund *1849–1928*
  Portraits from life.
  1. English literature, 1800–1900 – Biographies –
  Collections
  I. Title II. Thwaite, Ann
  820.9007

Library of Congress Cataloging-in-Publications Data
Gosse, Edmund, 1849–1928.
  Portraits from life / by Edmund Gosse; edited with an introduction by
Ann Thwaite.
    p. cm.
  Includes bibliographical references and index.
  ISBN 0–85967–796–6
  1. Authors, English–19th century–Biography. 2. Authors, American–19th
century–Biography. I. Thwaite, Ann. II. Title.
  PR105.G67 1991
820′.9–dc20
[B]   90–48108
            CIP

ISBN 0–85967–796–6

Phototypeset by Input Typesetting Ltd, London

Printed and bound in Great Britain by
Billing and Sons Limited, Worcester.

Contents

for
Michael Millgate and Alistair Elliot
with thanks

Introduction

As a very young man, Edmund Gosse dreamed of fame, of being among the English poets at his death. "What a vista opens before us, full of desire and danger," he wrote to his friend, John Blaikie, with whom he shared his first book of poems. *Madrigals, Songs and Sonnets* was published, with his father's help, in 1870, the year Edmund was 21. The book sold only 12 copies. "Consider how things went with Shelley, Keats, Coleridge," the young poet wrote at the time. He was not discouraged.

Forty years later, less optimistic, Edmund Gosse brought out his *Collected Poems* and prefaced them with his portrait by Sargent (which, like the other Sargent portraits mentioned in this book of Patmore and James can be seen in the National Portrait Gallery in London). "The picture was painted a quarter of a century ago," Gosse wrote in his 1911 introduction, "and it represents what I was, not what I am. But so do these verses, which I now leave to their fate."

Their fate was neglect, and eventually, except for a couple which survive in my biography and in one or two anthologies, total disappearance. Gosse deserves to survive, not as a poet but as a writer of prose and, most specifically, as a writer from his own experience. *Father and Son*, his account of his own childhood (which is also, of course, a portrait of his remarkable father), has been until now his only book which is still in print and readily available. It is much admired and much loved. But his most substantial biographies – the one of his father (1890, seventeen years before *Father and Son*), of John Donne (1899), of Coventry Patmore (1905), of Ibsen (1907) and Swinburne (1917) – are now rarely read. And nor are his shorter lives of Gray, Raleigh, Congreve, Jeremy Taylor, Sir Thomas Browne and others.

In addition to his biographical books, Gosse wrote dozens of short portraits. He relished "anecdotal history" and the thought of himself contributing to the biographical record of his own time. It is the intention of this book to revive and make easily accessible a number of Gosse's studies from life. He wrote in his preface to *Portraits and Sketches* (1912) that these studies were mostly "of authors whom I have known more or less intimately, and have observed with curiosity and imagination . . . They are imperfect, perhaps erroneous, but they are not secondhand". They are "drawn faithfully from the life". I used some of this material, of course, in my 1984 biography of Edmund Gosse, but most of it has not been readily available since Gosse's death in May 1928, more than 60 years ago.

One of the last things Gosse did was to write a preface (dated in the very month of his death) to a two-volume selection of his essays, published by Heinemann in their Travellers' Library. Gosse wrote:

> These two volumes have no didactic purpose. They were not written, and they are not re-issued, for purposes of instruction. There is a sense, of course, in which all statements of fact are liable to instruct the reader who comes to them for positive information. But my object has never been to teach. I have not the peculiar gift which the teacher needs. Let me say quite clearly that I have always been an artist and never a tutor. From an accident in my temperament for which I can give no reason, since my childhood I have been like the unhappy Emperor Julian, who also was not fitted to teach. As it was in his case, so in mine there has possessed me, *incidit desiderium*, an intense love of books and of the history of authors. The indulgence of this passion has been the joy of my life . . .

The editor of those two 1928 volumes mixed, as Gosse had himself in his own earlier collections, some criticism of long-dead writers (such as "The Charm of Sterne" and "The Challenge of the Brontës") and of individual books (for instance, *Les Liaisons Dangereuses*, then much less well-known than it is today) with literary essays on more general subjects. The editor selected 26 essays for the two books and only three of them (on Tennyson, Christina Rossetti and Horne) are portraits included now in this book. Yet it is these descriptions from the living flesh that still reward our attention.

Robert Louis Stevenson – himself the subject of the first portrait in my collection – once told Gosse to "see as many people as you can and make a book of them before you die. That will be a living book, upon my word." Gosse certainly "saw" a great many people. He could count among his closest friends many of the most eminent people of his time, not only writers but also politicians, peers and soldiers. He was extremely gregarious from those first days when he discovered friendship in Devon – "a glorious life among wild boys on the margin of the sea". As a young man he had a knack of making friends with the right people – the poets naturally included future poets laureate, the novelists the best novelists on both sides of the Atlantic, the schoolmasters would turn into masters of Cambridge colleges, the soldiers into commanders-in-chief, the politicians became cabinet ministers and even the few clergymen had bishop's mitres tucked under their surplices.

Gosse wrote mainly about the writers; their portraits can be found among much less interesting material in a number of out-of-print collections: *Critical Kit-Kats*, *Portraits and Sketches*, *Some Diversions of a Man of Letters*, *Aspects and Impressions* and so on. It is now over a hundred years since the earliest portrait included here – Gosse's memories of Browning – was published in the *New Review*. This book of mine is an attempt to make from this scattered material the sort of living book Stevenson was suggesting and which Gosse never made himself. My collection includes Swinburne and Patmore, two of the three men (the other was Leicester Warren, Lord de Tabley) whom Gosse named as the most formative influences on his intellectual life in his early years. Interestingly, all three of them were outsiders, poets who could never have been poets laureate.

Putting aside the parallels with the fourth-century Emperor Julian in that preface I quoted (which do not much illuminate the case for us), Gosse's denial of his role as a teacher is worth comment. Victorian literary critics were certainly expected to have a didactic role – indeed critics, and Gosse became largely known as a critic, have never been considered to be primarily artists or entertainers. For many years Gosse attempted to teach, in spite of his lack of any scholarly training and, in fact, of any formal education after the age of 17. (Gosse started work as a clerk in the library of the British Museum in January 1867, four years before his first sight of Tennyson, described in these pages.) As he said in the Preface I quoted, Gosse traced his inability as a teacher to some "accident in his temperament" from his childhood.

As a child, Edmund had spent long hours making his own books in a stuffy boxroom in the house in Devon. His *Zoological Sket-*

ches Consisting of Descriptions and Engravings of Animals were written and illustrated in the year he was nine and give little evidence of any remarkable early talent. They were, as he himself says in *Father and Son*, "ludicrous pastiches" of the work of his father, the distinguished marine biologist P H Gosse, who could not bear the child spending so much time on these pathetic parodies of his own work. He wanted the boy "not to copy him but to go out into the garden or the shore and describe something new, in a new way", to observe and to communicate with accuracy. It was his "genius for inaccuracy", as Henry James described it, that made Gosse unfitted to be a teacher. Certainly, readers who come to Gosse primarily for "positive information", for facts, might find themselves in trouble; but Gosse had to suffer a good deal, most notably over Churton Collins' attack on his Clark lectures in the *Quarterly Review*, before he came to accept that he was "never a tutor", in any sense of the word. The subject of his most effective observation and communication was not to be literary history (and not, of course, botanical or biological specimens from garden or seashore) but the people, mainly writers, who became his friends. The truth would come from his own experience, but even here his memory could let him down. I shall comment more on that aspect of his essays in the Notes.

As we saw, Edmund Gosse, at the end of his life, claimed to "have always been an artist". There has been much dispute about whether the biographer is entitled to make that claim. Desmond MacCarthy used the phrase "an artist on oath", and Virginia Woolf in 1927 saw that the biographer "chooses; he synthesises; in short, he has ceased to be the chronicler; he has become an artist". But when she returned to the subject of biography in an essay reprinted in *The Death of the Moth* (1942) she had changed her mind and decided that a biographer is "a craftsman, not an artist; and his work is not a work of art but something betwixt and between." An artist, she seems to say, cannot be "on oath", cannot have so much responsibility to facts. Gosse would rather, I am sure, not have had that responsibility. He would rather have been a poet. It is poets, above all, who fascinate him. Of the 12 portraits in this book, nine are of poets.

Malcolm Bradbury has commented on the fact that writing about writers is "something of a challenge, even a provocation" to the academic today, for

> literary study is not greatly to do with writers but with writing,
> not with authors but with texts, not with factual records but

4

with conceptual theory. And in this it seems to differ very largely from what goes on in what we call the "real" world. Here writers' lives are often found more interesting than writers' works.*

Biographies will quite regularly sell more copies than any actual book by the writer in question, as Bradbury comments. It would be interesting to know how many copies of Wilde's plays or *The Portrait of Dorian Gray* sold during the period when 90,000 copies were sold of Richard Ellmann's biography. I suspect it would have been considerably more than usual, and Gosse on Swinburne might even incline us to read a Swinburne poem for the first time in years. But by printing Gosse's portraits of "Orion" Horne and Wolcott Balestier I am acknowledging there are times when the writer has an interest quite beyond the one of illuminating his own texts.

Gosse was well aware of the dangers of readers being more interested in the artist than in his art. In his reflections after Tennyson's funeral (see p.53), he commented on the fact that "the world now expects its poets to be picturesque, as aged and as individual as he was, or else it will pay poetry no attention". That was a hundred years ago and the public still prefers its poets to behave, if not like Tennyson, at least in as "individual" a manner as Dylan Thomas, Robert Lowell or Allen Ginsberg, or to give the suggestion of mysteries under a conventional exterior, as in the cases of T S Eliot and Philip Larkin. The reading public has little time for deconstruction or the Death of the Author. If the academy likes to think of biography as a higher form of gossip, it can hardly deny, as Michael Millgate has suggested, that autobiography is "a sub-genre of fiction", and that both biography and autobiography can be as worthy of study as fiction itself.

Gosse did not, in fact, provide us with a real portrait of Tennyson, whom he did not know well. Nor, unfortunately, do we have a full-scale picture of Thomas Hardy, whom Gosse did know extremely well over a period of no fewer than 53 years, as he pointed out in the broadcast he made in February 1928 just after Hardy's death and only a short time before his own. They died within a few months of each other, and this is undoubtedly the reason Gosse did not attempt anything on the lines of the most important essays in this collection, on Stevenson, Browning and Henry James. Gosse loved them all. He loved Swinburne too

* "The telling life, some thoughts on literary biography", in *The Troubled Face of Biography*, Homberger & Charmley, 1988.

and wrote a similarly loving short portrait of him – the "most extraordinary" man he thought he had ever known. That was published in 1912, not long after Swinburne's death and when Gosse was beginning to write his full-scale biography, a book he published five years later after considerable problems. He heeded, in Desmond MacCarthy's words, reviewing the biography in the *New Statesman*, the "voice of that old Dame, Discretion, to whose warnings Mr Gosse in writing *Father and Son* was so fortunately deaf". In fact, the Swinburne family had laid a total embargo on "any mention of drunkenness" and "a still heavier sexual embargo". Three years later, Gosse lodged in the British Museum the *Confidential Paper*, which supplements the story in his biography and which I have decided to include here.

As Gosse said in his 1925 lecture on "Tallemant des Réaux or the Art of Miniature Biography", he had no time for the "marmoreal school" of biography, for hagiographers and deifiers. By then, after Lytton Strachey had published *Eminent Victorians*, things were looking rather different from the way they had a dozen years earlier, when Gosse had seen the danger of twentieth-century biography as its "unwillingness to accept any man's character save at the valuation of his most cautious relatives". As early as 1897, he had written in a letter: "If biographers would only see how much they enhance the qualities of their subjects by admitting peculiarities and even failings." If, as Harold Nicolson would suggest, biography was replacing theology, as people turned from God to human experience, the last thing readers wanted was "the goody-goody lives of good men". The characters who interest us most are those whose weaknesses we recognize in ourselves. But Swinburne's failings and weaknesses were too remarkable for Gosse to feel any account of them could be published while relatives remained alive. He left the true record for posterity, for us.

Writing about Tallemant, Gosse admired the way he was "not occupied with vice or virtue, save as they are elements in the composition of the picture". Tallemant's portraits were not published in his lifetime. He wrote, Gosse said, "with no apparent purpose whatever save the pleasure of a solitary artist in his work." But Gosse generally wrote for an audience, not for himself, and so had to accommodate the taste of his time.

Perhaps it is not too fanciful to imagine Edmund Gosse, as he imagined Tallemant, stealing noiselessly from his place in his drawing-room, going up to his own room, sitting at his desk and scribbling in a volume, "before a word of it could fade from his memory, the latest juicy malignity or prime illuminating anecdote." The picture is not quite convincing for Gosse himself, if only because we know that his desk, his study, in Hanover Terrace was a part of the very room where his guests enjoyed themselves. Certainly Gosse was more a participant, less a simple witness. Tallemant often wrote from the talk of the town, sometimes about people he had probably never met. Gosse rarely did this. The most notable example is his essay on George Eliot in *Aspects and Impressions*, in which he sees her passing in a victoria with Lewes and again, just before her death, "tightening round her shoulders a white wool shawl", in the audience at a concert in the Langham Hall. I have not included this piece, for these impressions, though vivid, are not sufficient to make the essay a 'portrait from life''. All the portraits here are from a closer personal contact than that. Indeed Walt Whitman, for obvious geographical reasons, is the only one with whom Gosse's contact was brief. Lady Dorothy Nevill is the only subject who is not a writer. She seems worth including as representative of a considerable number of women with whom Gosse had close friendships, from Isabel Becker and Elise Otté, remarkable friends of his youth, to a cluster of aristocrats in the last years of his life.

It is Gosse's curiosity and eye for detail that make all these portraits so vivid. In his review of a biography of Samuel Butler, Gosse said that Festing Jones assures the reader "that Butler took eight handkerchiefs and three pairs of socks with him when he went abroad" (one immediately wonders about the length of his stay) "and that he very wisely carried diarrhoea pills in the handle half of his Gladstone bag." Gosse realizes that there may be readers who do not care how many times Butler brushed his hair every day, but he was not one of them. "These little things," he said, "are my delight."

In these pages, readers will find few things of as small moment as socks and handkerchiefs, but plenty of little things to delight: Stevenson playing a silent game of chess with Gosse on the coverlet of his bed at Braemar, preserving his voice for the evening's reading of what was to be *Treasure Island*; Christina Rossetti in an "extraordinarily ordinary skirt"; Browning recalling a headache he had had in St Petersburg more than 50 years before; Henry James patting small heads in Rye.

If we regret we were born too late to meet Stevenson or James, with Swinburne or Patmore we can certainly feel they are more agreeable to read about than to cope with in real life. Gosse had to experience anguish and confusion and the alternating excitement and tedium involved in any friendship with the

7

alcoholic Swinburne. Patmore could be tedious too, "winking, blinking, smoking innumerable cigarettes and saying next to nothing" or "withering conversation by some paradox". Gosse worked hard for some of the material in these portraits but what survives is his enjoyment and sympathy, his zest for life and friendship which permeates all his writing.

Ann Thwaite
Low Tharston, Norfolk

Note on style

Gosse and his various publishers were of course not consistent about punctuation and style, particularly over such things as whether titles should be in italics or inverted commas. My general policy (while adding a few omitted letters and correcting some obvious slips) has been to leave things as they were on original publication. Sometimes (as on p. 74 with *Justine*) two styles appear on one page.

AT

Robert Louis Stevenson
1850–1894

This essay comes from *Critical Kit-Kats*, a collection of essays Gosse published in 1896, the same year as Stevenson's last unfinished book, *Weir of Hermiston*. It originally appeared in the *Century Magazine* in July 1895. Stevenson and Gosse had kept closely in touch during Stevenson's years in Samoa, though sometimes letters would go astray, and Stevenson once said he felt he was writing "to feed the maw" of Sydney Post Office, through which letters to and from Samoa were routed. In 1894 Gosse dedicated his book of poems *In Russet and Silver* to Stevenson, under the name Tusitala, the story-teller. It includes a reference to their first meeting, recalled also at the beginning of this essay:

> Ah! but does your heart remember, Tusitala,
> Westward in our Scotch September
> Blue against the pale sun's ember, –
> That low rim of faint long islands,
> Barren granite-snouted nesses
> Plunging in the dull'd Atlantic,
> Where beyond Tiree one guesses
> At the full tide, loud and frantic?

The long poem is dated September 1894, and so remarkably speedy was publishing and the post that the book reached Stevenson on his Pacific Island in time for him to write and thank Gosse on the following 1 December. The letter was perhaps the last he wrote. Two days later, quite unexpectedly (in spite of the prophetic ending), Stevenson was dead. He had written words that contrast movingly with words he had used years earlier (and which Gosse quotes in his essay), at a time when the path was "most of it uphill", with the hill catching the breath and the brambles tearing at the face and hands. At what was the end of his life, Stevenson wrote to Gosse:

I have, in fact, lost the path that makes it easy for you to descend

9

the hill. I am going at it straight. And where I have to go down it is a precipice . . .

May you write many more books as good as this one – only there's one thing impossible, you can never write another dedication that can give the same pleasure to the vanished

Tusitala.

Long before the letter arrived in London, Robert Louis Stevenson had indeed vanished; his body had been borne on the shoulders of his Samoan friends to its last resting place high on Mount Vaea. Gosse wrote to his daughter, Tessa, of Stevenson's last letter: "I feel as if it was almost the very most precious thing I possess, this goodbye from the great genius that I loved so much."

*　　*　　*

It is nearly a quarter of a century since I first saw Stevenson. In the autumn of 1870, in company with a former schoolfellow, I was in the Hebrides. We had been wandering in the Long Island, as they name the outer archipelago, and our steamer, returning, called at Skye. At the pier of Portree, I think, a company came on board – "people of importance in their day," Edinburgh acquaintances, I suppose, who had accidentally met in Skye on various errands. At all events, they invaded our modest vessel with a loud sound of talk. Professor Blackie was among them, a famous figure that calls for no description; and a voluble, shaggy man, clad in homespun, with spectacles forward upon nose, who, it was whispered to us, was Mr Sam Bough, the Scottish Academician, a water-colour painter of some repute, who was to die in 1878. There were also several engineers of prominence. At the tail of this chatty, jesting little crowd of invaders came a youth of about my own age, whose appearance, for some mysterious reason, instantly attracted me. He was tall, preternaturally lean, with longish hair, and as restless and questing as a spaniel. The party from Portree fairly took possession of us; at meals they crowded around the captain, and we common tourists sat silent, below the salt. The stories of Blackie and Sam Bough were resonant. Meanwhile, I knew not why, I watched the plain, pale lad who took the lowest place in this privileged company.

The summer of 1870 remains in the memory of western Scotland as one of incomparable splendour. Our voyage, especially as evening drew on, was like an emperor's progress. We stayed on deck

10

till the latest moment possible, and I occasionally watched the lean youth, busy and serviceable, with some of the little tricks with which we were later on to grow familiar – the advance with hand on hip, the sidewise bending of the head to listen. Meanwhile darkness overtook us, a wonderful halo of moonlight swam up over Glenelg, the indigo of the peaks of the Cuchullins faded into the general blue night. I went below, but was presently aware of some change of course, and then of an unexpected stoppage. I tore on deck, and found that we had left our track among the islands, and had steamed up a narrow and unvisited fiord of the mainland – I think Loch Nevis. The sight was curious and bewildering. We lay in a gorge of blackness, with only a strip of the blue moonlit sky overhead; in the dark a few lanterns jumped about the shore, carried by agitated but unseen and soundless persons. As I leaned over the bulwarks, Stevenson was at my side, and he explained to me that we had come up this loch to take away to Glasgow a large party of emigrants driven from their homes in the interests of a deer-forest. As he spoke, a black mass became visible entering the vessel. Then, as we slipped off shore, the fact of their hopeless exile came home to these poor fugitives, and suddenly, through the absolute silence, there rose from them a wild keening and wailing, reverberated by the cliffs of the loch, and at that strange place and hour infinitely poignant. When I came on deck next morning, my unnamed friend was gone. He had put off with the engineers to visit some remote lighthouse of the Hebrides.

This early glimpse of Stevenson is a delightful memory to me. When we met next, not only did I instantly recall him, but, what was stranger, he remembered me. This voyage in the *Clansman* was often mentioned between us, and it has received for me a sort of consecration from the fact that in the very last letter that Louis wrote, finished on the day of his death, he made a reference to it.

*

. . . It was in 1877, or late in 1876, that I was presented to Stevenson, at the old Savile Club, by Mr Sidney Colvin, who thereupon left us to our devices. We went downstairs and lunched together, and then we adjourned to the smoking-room. As twilight came on I tore myself away, but Stevenson walked with me across Hyde Park, and nearly to my house. He had an engagement, and so had I, but I walked a mile or two back with him. The fountains

11

of talk had been unsealed, and they drowned the conventions. I came home dazzled with my new friend, saying, as Constance does of Arthur, "Was ever such a gracious creature born?" That impression of ineffable mental charm was formed at the first moment of acquaintance, and it never lessened or became modified. Stevenson's rapidity in the sympathetic interchange of ideas was, doubtless, the source of it. He has been described as an "egotist", but I challenge the description. If ever there was an altruist, it was Louis Stevenson; he seemed to feign an interest in himself merely to stimulate you to be liberal in your confidences.*

Those who have written about him from later impressions than those of which I speak seem to me to give insufficient prominence to the gaiety of Stevenson. It was his cardinal quality in those early days. A childlike mirth leaped and danced in him; he seemed to skip upon the hills of life. He was simply bubbling with quips and jests; his inherent earnestness or passion about abstract things was incessantly relieved by jocosity; and when he had built one of his intellectual castles in the sand, a wave of humour was certain to sweep in and destroy it. I cannot, for the life of me, recall any of his jokes; and written down in cold blood, they might not be funny if I did. They were not wit so much as humanity, the many-sided outlook upon life. I am anxious that his laughter-loving mood should not be forgotten, because later on it was partly, but I think never wholly, quenched by ill health, responsibility, and the advance of years. He was often, in the old days, excessively and delightfully silly – silly with the silliness of an inspired schoolboy; and I am afraid that our laughter sometimes sounded ill in the ears of age.

A pathos was given to his gaiety by the fragility of his health. He was never well, all the years I knew him; and we looked upon his life as hanging by the frailest tenure. As he never complained or maundered, this, no doubt – though we were not aware of it – added to the charm of his presence. He was so bright and keen and witty, and any week he might die. No one, certainly, conceived it possible that he could reach his forty-fifth year. In 1879 his health visibly began to run lower, and he used to bury himself in lonely Scotch and French places, "tinkering himself with solitude," as he used to say.

---

* This continued to be his characteristic to the last. Thus he described an interview he had in Sydney with some man formerly connected with the "black-birding" trade, by saying: "He was very shy at first, and it was not till I told him of a good many of my escapades that I could get him to thaw, and then he poured it all out. I have always found that the best way of getting people to be confidential."

My experience of Stevenson during these first years was confined to London, upon which he would make sudden piratical descents, staying a few days or weeks, and melting into air again. He was much at my house; and it must be told that my wife and I, as young married people, had possessed ourselves of a house too large for our slender means immediately to furnish. The one person who thoroughly approved of our great, bare, absurd drawing-room was Louis, who very earnestly dealt with us on the immorality of chairs and tables, and desired us to sit always, as he delighted to sit, upon hassocks on the floor. Nevertheless, as arm-chairs and settees straggled into existence, he handsomely consented to use them, although never in the usual way, but with his legs thrown sidewise over the arms of them, or the head of a sofa treated as a perch. In particular, a certain shelf, with cupboards below, attached to a bookcase, is worn with the person of Stevenson, who would spend half an evening while passionately discussing some great question of morality or literature, leaping sidewise in a seated posture to the length of this shelf, and then back again. He was eminently peripatetic too, and never better company than walking in the street, this exercise seeming to inflame his fancy. But his most habitual dwelling-place in the London of those days was the Savile Club, then lodged in an inconvenient but very friendly house in Savile Row. Louis pervaded the club; he was its most affable and chatty member; and he lifted it, by the ingenuity of his incessant dialectic, to the level of a sort of humorous Academe or Mouseion.

At this time he must not be thought of as a successful author. A very few of us were convinced of his genius; but with the exception of Mr Leslie Stephen, nobody of editorial status was sure of it. I remember the publication of *An Inland Voyage* in 1878, and the inability of the critics and the public to see anything unusual in it.

Stevenson was not without a good deal of innocent oddity in his dress. When I try to conjure up his figure, I can see only a slight, lean lad, in a suit of blue sea-cloth, a black shirt, and a wisp of yellow carpet that did duty for a necktie. This was long his attire, persevered in to the anguish of his more conventional acquaintances. I have a ludicrous memory of going, in 1878, to buy him a new hat, in company with Mr Lang, the thing then upon his head having lost the semblance of a human article of dress. Aided by a very civil shopman, we suggested several hats and caps, and Louis at first seemed interested; but having presently hit upon one which appeared to us pleasing and decorous, we

13

turned for a moment to inquire the price. We turned back, and found that Louis had fled, the idea of parting with the shapeless object having proved too painful to be entertained. By the way, Mr Lang will pardon me if I tell, in exacter detail, a story of his. It was immediately after the adventure with the hat that, not having quite enough money to take him from London to Edinburgh, third class, he proposed to the railway clerk to throw in a copy of Mr Swinburne's *Queen-Mother and Rosamond*. The offer was refused with scorn, although the book was of the first edition, and even then worth more than the cost of a whole ticket.

Stevenson's pity was a very marked quality, and it extended to beggars, which is, I think, to go too far. His optimism, however, suffered a rude shock in South Audley Street one summer afternoon. We met a stalwart beggar, whom I refused to aid. Louis, however, wavered, and finally handed him sixpence. The man pocketed the coin, forbore to thank his benefactor, but, fixing his eye on me, said, in a loud voice, "And what is the other little gentleman going to give me?" "In future," said Louis, as we strode coldly on, "*I* shall be 'the other little gentleman.' "

In those early days he suffered many indignities on account of his extreme youthfulness of appearance and absence of self-assertion. He was at Inverness – being five or six and twenty at the time – and had taken a room in a hotel. Coming back about dinner-time, he asked the hour of table d'hôte, whereupon the landlady said, in a motherly way: "Oh, I knew you wouldn't like to sit in there among the grown-up people, so I've had a place put for you in the bar." There was a frolic at the Royal Hotel, Bathgate, in the summer of 1879. Louis was lunching alone, and the maid, considering him a negligible quantity, came and leaned out of the window. This outrage on the proprieties was so stinging that Louis at length made free to ask her, with irony, what she was doing there. "I'm looking for my lad," she replied. "Is that he?" asked Stevenson, with keener sarcasm. "Weel, I've been lookin' for him a' my life, and I've never seen him yet," was the response. Louis was disarmed at once, and wrote her on the spot some beautiful verses in the vernacular. "They're no bad for a beginner," she was kind enough to say when she had read them.

The year 1879 was a dark one in the life of Louis. He had formed a conviction that it was his duty to go out to the extreme west of the United States, while his family and the inner circle of his friends were equally certain that it was neither needful nor expedient that he should make this journey. As it turned out, they were wrong, and he was right; but in the circumstances their

14

opinion seemed the only correct one. His health was particularly bad, and he was ordered, not West, but South. The expedition, which he has partly described in *The Amateur Emigrant* and *Across the Plains*, was taken, therefore, in violent opposition to all those whom he left in England and Scotland; and this accounts for the mode in which it was taken. He did not choose to ask for money to be spent in going to California, and it was hoped that the withdrawal of supplies would make the voyage impossible. But Louis, bringing to the front a streak of iron obstinacy which lay hidden somewhere in his gentle nature, scraped together enough to secure him a steerage passage across the Atlantic.

The day before he started he spent with my wife and me – a day of stormy agitation, an April day of rain-clouds and sunshine; for it was not in Louis to remain long in any mood. I seem to see him now, pacing the room, a cigarette spinning in his wasted fingers. To the last we were trying to dissuade him from what seemed to us the maddest of enterprises. He was so ill that I did not like to leave him, and at night – it was midsummer weather – we walked down into town together. We were by this time, I suppose, in a pretty hysterical state of mind, and as we went through Berkeley Square, in mournful discussion of the future, Louis suddenly proposed that we should visit the so-called "Haunted House," which then occupied the newspapers. The square was quiet in the decency of a Sunday evening. We found the house, and one of us boldly knocked at the door. There was no answer and no sound, and we jeered upon the door-step; but suddenly we were both aware of a pale face – a phantasm in the dusk – gazing down upon us from a surprising height. It was the caretaker, I suppose, mounted upon a flight of steps: but terror gripped us at the heart, and we fled with footsteps as precipitate as those of schoolboys caught in an orchard. I think that ghostly face in Berkeley Square must have been Louis's latest European impression for many months.

*

All the world now knows, through the two books which I have named, what immediately happened. Presently letters began to arrive, and in one from Monterey, written early in October 1879, he told me of what was probably the nearest approach of death that ever came until the end, fifteen years later. I do not think it is generally known, even in the inner circle of his friends, that in September of that year he was violently ill, alone, at an Angora-goat ranch in the Santa Lucia Mountains. "I scarcely slept or ate or thought for four days," he said. "Two nights I lay out under a tree, in a sort of stupor, doing nothing but fetch water for myself and horse, light a fire and make coffee, and all night awake hearing the goat-bells ringing and the tree-toads singing, when each new noise was enough to set me mad." Then an old frontiersman, a mighty hunter of bears, came round, and tenderly nursed him through his attack. "By all rule this should have been my death; but after a while my spirit got up again in a divine frenzy, and has since kicked and spurred my vile body forward with great emphasis and success."

Late in the winter of 1879, with renewed happiness and calm of life, and also under the spur of a need of money, he wrote with much assiduity. Among other things, he composed at Monterey the earliest of his novels, a book called *A Vendetta in the West*, the manuscript of which seems to have disappeared. Perhaps we need not regret it; for, so he declared to me, "It was about as bad as Ouida, but not quite, for it was not so eloquent." He had made a great mystery of his whereabouts; indeed, for several months no one was to know what had become of him, and his letters were to be considered secret. At length, in writing from Monterey, on November 15, 1879, he removed the embargo: "That I am in California may now be published to the brethren." In the summer of the next year, after a winter of very serious ill health, during which more than once he seemed on the brink of a galloping consumption, he returned to England. He had married in California a charming lady whom we all soon learned to regard as the most appropriate and helpful companion that Louis could possibly have secured. On October 8, 1880 – a memorable day – he made his first appearance in London since his American exile. A post-card from Edinburgh had summoned me to "appoint with an appointment" certain particular friends; "and let us once again," Louis wrote, "lunch together in the Savile Halls." Mr Lang and Mr Walter Pollock, and, I think, Mr Henley, graced the occasion, and the club cellar produced a bottle of Chambertin of quite uncommon merit. Louis, I may explain, had a peculiar passion for Burgundy, which he esteemed the wine of highest possibilities in the whole Bacchic order; and I have often known him descant on a Pommard or a Montrachet in terms so exquisite that the listeners could scarcely taste the wine itself.

Davos-Platz was now prescribed for the rickety lungs; and late in that year Louis and his wife took up their abode there, at the Hôtel Buol, he carrying with him a note from me recommending

16

him to the care of John Addington Symonds. Not at first, but presently and on the whole, these two men, so singular in their generation, so unique and so unlike, "hit it off," as people say, and were an intellectual solace to each other; but their real friendship did not begin till a later year. I remember Stevenson saying to me next spring that to be much with Symonds was to "adventure in a thornwood." It was at Davos, this winter of 1880, that Stevenson took up the study of Hazlitt, having found a publisher who was willing to bring out a critical and biographical memoir. This scheme occupied a great part of Louis's attention, but was eventually dropped; for the further he progressed in the investigation of Hazlitt's character the less he liked it, and the squalid *Liber Amoris* gave the *coup de grâce*. He did not know what he would be at. His vocation was not yet apparent to him. He talked of writing on craniology and the botany of the Alps. The unwritten books of Stevenson will one day attract the scholiast, who will endeavour, perhaps, to reconstruct them from the references to them in his correspondence. It may, therefore, be permissible to record here that he was long proposing to write a life of the Duke of Wellington, for which he made some considerable collections. This was even advertised as "in preparation," on several occasions, from 1885 until 1887, but was ultimately abandoned. I remember his telling me that he intended to give emphasis to the "humour" of Wellington.

In June, 1881, we saw him again; but he passed very rapidly through London to a cottage at Pitlochry in Perthshire. He had lost his hold on town. "London," he wrote me, "now chiefly means to me Colvin and Henley, Leslie Stephen and you." He was now coursing a fresh literary hare, and set Mr Austin Dobson, Mr Saintsbury, and me busily hunting out facts about Jean Cavalier, the romantic eighteenth-century adventurer, whose life he fancied that he would write. His thoughts had recurred, in fact, to Scottish history; and he suddenly determined to do what seemed rather a mad thing – namely, to stand for the Edinburgh professorship of history, then just vacant. We were all whipped up for testimonials, and a little pamphlet exists, in a pearl-grey cover – the despair of bibliophiles – in which he and a strange assortment of his friends set forth his claims. These required nimble treatment, since, to put it plainly, it was impossible to say that he had any. His appeal was treated by the advocates, who were the electing body, with scant consideration, and some worthy gentleman was elected. The round Louis was well out of such a square hole as a chair in a university.

17

But something better was at hand. It was now, and in the peace of the Highlands, that Louis set out to become a popular writer. The fine art of "booming" had not then been introduced, nor the race of those who week by week discover coveys of fresh geniuses. Although Stevenson, in a sporadic way, had written much that was delightful, and that will last, he was yet – now at the close of his thirty-first year – by no means successful. The income he made by his pen was still ridiculously small; and Mr John Morley, amazing as it sounds to-day, had just refused to give him a book to write in the *English Men of Letters* series, on the ground of his obscurity as an author. All this was to be changed, and the book that was to do it was even now upon the stocks. In August the Stevensons moved to a house in Braemar – a place, as Louis said, "patronised by the royalty of the Sister Kingdoms – Victoria and the Cairngorms, sir, honouring that country-side by their conjunct presence." Hither I was invited, and here I paid an ever memorable visit. The house, as Louis was careful to instruct me, was entitled "The Cottage, late the late Miss McGregor's, Castleton of Braemar"; and thus I obediently addressed my letters until Louis remarked that "the reference to a deceased Highland lady, tending as it does to foster unavailing sorrow, may be with advantage omitted from the address."

To the Cottage, therefore, heedless of the manes of the late Miss McGregor, I proceeded in the most violent storm of hail and rain that even Aberdeenshire can produce in August, and found Louis as frail as a ghost, indeed, but better than I expected. He had adopted a trick of stretching his thin limbs over the back of a wicker sofa, which gave him an extraordinary resemblance to that quaint insect, the praying mantis; but it was a mercy to find him out of bed at all. Among the many attractions of the Cottage, the presence of Mr Thomas Stevenson – Louis's father – must not be omitted. He was then a singularly charming and vigorous personality, indignantly hovering at the borders of old age ("Sixty-three, sir, this year; and, deuce take it! am I to be called 'an old gentleman' by a cab-driver in the streets of Aberdeen?") and, to my gratitude and delight, my companion in long morning walks. The detestable weather presently brought all the other members of the household to their beds, and Louis in particular became a wreck. However, it was a wreck that floated every day at nightfall; for at the worst he was able to come down-stairs to dinner and spend the evening with us.

We passed the days with regularity. After breakfast I went to Louis's bedroom, where he sat up in bed, with dark, flashing eyes and ruffled hair, and we played chess on the coverlet. Not a word passed, for he was strictly forbidden to speak in the early part of the day. As soon as he felt tired – often in the middle of a game – he would rap with peremptory knuckles on the board as a signal to stop, and then Mrs Stevenson or I would arrange his writing materials on the bed. Then I would see no more of him till dinner-time, when he would appear, smiling and voluble, the horrid bar of speechlessness having been let down. Then every night, after dinner, he would read us what he had written during the day. I find in a note to my wife, dated September 3, 1881: "Louis has been writing, all the time I have been here, a novel of pirates and hidden treasure, in the highest degree exciting. He reads it to us every night, chapter by chapter." This, of course, was *Treasure Island*, about the composition of which, long afterward, in Samoa, he wrote an account in some parts of which I think that his memory played him false. I look back to no keener intellectual pleasure than those cold nights at Braemar, with the sleet howling outside, and Louis reading his budding romance by the lamplight, emphasizing the purpler passages with lifted voice and gesticulating finger.

*

Hardly had I left the Cottage than the harsh and damp climate of Aberdeenshire was felt to be rapidly destroying Louis, and he and his wife fled for Davos. Before the end of October they were ensconced there in a fairly comfortable châlet. Here Louis and his step-son amused themselves by setting up a hand-press, which Mr Osbourne worked, and for which Louis provided the literary material. Four or five laborious little publications were put forth, some of them illustrated by the daring hand of Stevenson himself. He complained to me that Mr Osbourne was a very ungenerous publisher – "one penny a cut, and one halfpenny a set of verses. What do you say to that for Grub Street?" These little diversions were brought to a close by the printer-publisher breaking, at one fell swoop, the press and his own finger. The little "Davos Press" issues now fetch extravagant prices, which would have filled author and printer with amazement. About this time Louis and I had a good deal of correspondence about a work which he had proposed that we should undertake in collaboration – a retelling, in choice literary form, of the most picturesque murder cases of the last hundred years. We were to visit the scenes of these crimes, and turn over the evidence. The great thing, Louis said, was not to begin to write until we were thoroughly alarmed. "These things must be done, my boy, under the very shudder of the goose-flesh." We were to begin with the "Story of the Red Barn," which indeed is a tale pre-eminently worthy to be retold by Stevenson. But the scheme never came off, and is another of the dead leaves in his Vallombrosa.

We saw him in London again, for a few days, in October 1882; but this was a melancholy period. For eight months at the close of that year and the beginning of 1883 he was capable of no mental exertion. He was in the depths of languor, and in nightly apprehension of a fresh attack. He slept excessively, and gave humorous accounts of the drowsiness that hung upon him, addressing his notes as "from the Arms of Porpus" (Morpheus) and "at the Sign of the Poppy." No climate seemed to relieve him, and so, in the autumn of 1882, a bold experiment was tried. As the snows of Davos were of no avail, the hot, damp airs of Hyères should be essayed. I am inclined to dwell in some fulness on the year he spent at Hyères because, curiously enough, it was not so much as mentioned, to my knowledge, by any of the writers of obituary notices at Stevenson's death. It takes, nevertheless, a prominent place in his life's history, for his removal thither marked a sudden and brilliant, though only temporary, revival in his health and spirits. Some of his best work, too, was written at Hyères, and one might say that fame first found him in this warm corner of southern France.

The house at Hyères was called "La Solitude." It stood in a paradise of roses and aloes, fig-marigolds and olives. It had delectable and even, so Louis declared, "sub-celestial" views over a plain bounded by "certain mountains as graceful as Apollo, as severe as Zeus"; and at first the hot mistral, which blew and burned where it blew, seemed the only drawback. Not a few of the best poems in the *Underwoods* reflect the ecstasy of convalescence under the skies and perfumes of La Solitude. By the summer Louis could report "good health of a radiant order." It was while he was at Hyères that Stevenson first directly addressed an American audience, and I may record that, in September 1883, he told me to "beg Gilder your prettiest for a gentleman in pecuniary sloughs." Mr Gilder was quite alive to the importance of securing such a contributor, although when the Amateur Emigrant had entered the office of *The Century Magazine* in 1879 he had been very civilly but coldly shown the door. (I must be allowed to tease my good friends in Union Square by recording that fact!) Mr

Gilder asked for fiction, but received instead *The Silverado Squatters*, which duly appeared in the magazine.

It was also arranged that Stevenson should make an ascent of the Rhône for *The Century* . . . Abruptly, however, in January 1884, another crisis came. He went to Nice, where he was thought to be dying. He saw no letters; all his business was kindly taken charge of by Mr Henley; and again, for a long time, he passed beneath the penumbra of steady languor and infirmity. When it is known how constantly he suffered, how brief and flickering were the intervals of comparative health, it cannot but add to the impression of his radiant fortitude through all these trials, and of his persistent employment of all his lucid moments. It was pitiful, and yet at the same time very inspiriting, to see a creature so feeble and so ill equipped for the struggle bear himself so smilingly and so manfully through all his afflictions. There can be no doubt, however, that this latest breakdown vitally affected his spirits. He was never, after this, quite the gay child of genius that he had previously been. Something of a graver cast became natural to his thoughts; he had seen Death in the cave. And now for the first time we traced a new note in his writings – the note of "Pulvis et Umbra."

After 1883 my personal memories of Stevenson become very casual. In November 1884, he was settled at Bournemouth, in a villa called Bonaltie Towers, and there he stayed until, in March 1885, he took a house of his own, which, in pious memory of his grandfather, he named Skerryvore . . . To my constant sorrow, I was never able to go to Bournemouth during the years he lived there. It has been described to me, by those who were more fortunate, as a pleasure that was apt to tantalize and evade the visitor, so constantly was the invalid unable, at the last, to see the friend who had travelled a hundred miles to speak with him. It was therefore during his visits to London, infrequent as these were, that we saw him at his best, for these were made at moments of unusual recovery. He generally lodged at what he called the "Monument," this being his title for Mr Colvin's house, a wing of the vast structure of the British Museum. I recall an occasion on which Louis dined with us (March 1886), because of the startling interest in the art of strategy which he had developed – an interest which delayed the meal with arrangements of serried bottles counter-scarped and lines of cruets drawn up on horseback ready to charge. So infectious was his enthusiasm that we forgot our hunger, and hung over the embattled table-cloth, easily persuaded to agree with him that neither poetry nor the plastic arts could compete for a moment with "the finished conduct, sir, of a large body of men in face of the enemy."

It was a little later that he took up the practice of modelling clay figures as he sat up in bed. Some of these compositions – which needed, perhaps, his eloquent commentary to convey their full effect to the spectator – were not without a measure of skill of design. I recollect his saying, with extreme gravity, "I am in sculpture what Mr Watts is in painting. We are both of us pre-occupied with moral and abstract ideas." I wonder whether any one has preserved specimens of these allegorical groups of clay.

The last time I had the happiness of seeing Stevenson was on Sunday, August 21, 1887. He had been brought up from Bournem-outh the day before in a wretched condition of health, and was lodged in a private hotel in Finsbury Circus, in the City, ready to be easily moved to a steamer in the Thames on the morrow. I was warned, in a note, of his passage through town, and of the uncertainty whether he could be seen. On the chance, I went over early on the 21st, and, very happily for me, he had had a fair night, and could see me for an hour or two. No one else but Mrs Stevenson was with him. His position was one which might have daunted any man's spirit, doomed to exile, in miserable health, starting vaguely across the Atlantic, with all his domestic interests rooted up, and with no notion where, or if at all, they should be replanted. If ever a man of imagination could be excused for repining, it was now.

But Louis showed no white feather. He was radiantly humorous and romantic. It was church time, and there was some talk of my witnessing his will, which I could not do, because there could be found no other reputable witness, the whole crew of the hotel being at church. This set Louis off on a splendid dream of romance. "This," he said, "is the way in which our valuable city hotels – packed, doubtless, with rich objects of jewellery – are deserted on a Sunday morning. Some bold piratical fellow, defying the spirit of Sabbatarianism, might make a handsome revenue by sacking the derelict hotels between the hours of ten and twelve. One hotel a week would suffice to enable such a man to retire into private life within the space of a year. A mask might, perhaps, be worn for the mere fancy of the thing, and to terrify kitchen-maids, but no real disguise would be needful to an enterprise that would require nothing but a brave heart and a careful study of the City Postal Directory." He spoke of the matter with so much fire and gallantry that I blushed for the youth of England and its lack of manly enterprise. No one ever could describe preposterous conduct with such a convincing air as Louis could. Common sense was positively humbled in his presence.

The volume of his poems called *Underwoods* had just appeared, and he inscribed a copy of it to me in the words "at Todgers', as ever was, *chez Todgers*, Pecksniff street." The only new book he seemed to wish to carry away with him was Mr Hardy's beautiful romance, *The Woodlanders*, which we had to scour London that Sunday afternoon to get hold of. In the evening Mr Colvin and I each returned to "Todgers'" with the three volumes, borrowed or stolen somewhere, and wrapped up for the voyage next day. And so the following morning, in an extraordinary vessel called the *Ludgate Hill*, carrying, besides the Stevensons, a cargo of stallions and monkeys, Mr and Mrs Stevenson and Mr Lloyd Osbourne steamed down the Thames in search of health across the Atlantic and the Pacific. The horses, Louis declared, protruded their noses in an unmannerly way between the passengers at dinner, and the poor little grey monkeys, giving up life for a bad job on board that strange, heaving cage, died by dozens, and were flung contemptuously out into the ocean. The strangest voyage, however, some time comes to an end, and Louis landed in America. He was never to cross the Atlantic again; and for those who loved him in Europe he had already journeyed more than half-way to another world.

*

It is impossible to deal, however lightly, with the personal qualities of Robert Louis Stevenson without dwelling on the extreme beauty of his character. In looking back over the twenty years in which I knew him, I feel that, since he was eminently human, I ought to recall his faults, but I protest that I can remember none. Perhaps the nearest approach to a fault was a certain want of discretion, always founded on a wish to make people understand each other, but not exactly according to wisdom. I recollect that he once embroiled me for a moment with John Addington Symonds in a manner altogether bloodthirsty and ridiculous, so that we both fell upon him and rended him. This little weakness is really the blackest crime I can lay to his charge. And on the other side, what courage, what love, what an indomitable spirit, what a melting pity! He had none of the sordid errors of the little man who writes – no sick ambition, no envy of others, no exaggeration of the value of this ephemeral trick of scribbling. He was eager to help his fellows, ready to take a second place, with

23

great difficulty offended, by the least show of repentance perfectly appeased.

Quite early in his career he adjusted himself to the inevitable sense of physical failure. He threw away from him all the useless impediments: he sat loosely in the saddle of life. Many men who get such a warning as he got take up something to lean against; according to their education or temperament, they support their maimed existence on religion, or on cynical indifference, or on some mania of the collector or the *dilettante*. Stevenson did none of these things. He determined to make the sanest and most genial use of so much of life as was left him. As any one who reads his books can see, he had a deep strain of natural religion; but he kept it to himself; he made no hysterical or ostentatious use of it.

Looking back at the past, one recalls a trait that had its significance, though one missed its meaning then. He was careful, as I have hardly known any other man to be, not to allow himself to be burdened by the weight of material things. It was quite a jest with us that he never acquired any possessions. In the midst of those who produced books, pictures, prints, bric-à-brac, none of these things ever stuck to Stevenson. There are some deep-sea creatures, the early part of whose life is spent dancing through the waters; at length some sucker or tentacle touches a rock, adheres, pulls down more tentacles, until the creature is caught there, stationary for the remainder of its existence. So it happens to men, and Stevenson's friends, one after another, caught the ground with a house, a fixed employment, a "stake in life;" he alone kept dancing in the free element, unattached. I remember his saying to me that if ever he had a garden he should like it to be empty, just a space to walk and talk in, with no flowers to need a gardener nor fine lawns that had to be mown. Just a fragment of the bare world to move in, that was all Stevenson asked for. And we who gathered possessions around us – a little library of rare books, a little gallery of drawings or bronzes – he mocked us with his goblin laughter; it was only so much more luggage to carry on the march, he said, so much more to strain the arms and bend the back.

Stevenson thought, as we all must think, that literature is a delightful profession, a primrose path. I remember his once saying so to me, and then he turned, with the brimming look in his lustrous eyes and the tremulous smile on his lips, and added, "But it is not all primroses, some of it is brambly, and most of it uphill." He knew – no one better – how the hill catches the breath

24

and how the brambles tear the face and hands; but he pushed strenuously, serenely on, searching for new paths, struggling to get up into the light and air.

One reason why it was difficult to be certain that Stevenson had reached his utmost in any direction was what I will call, for want of a better phrase, the *energetic modesty* of his nature. He was never satisfied with himself, yet never cast down. There are two dangers that beset the artist – the one is being pleased with what he has done, and the other being dejected with it. Stevenson, more than any other man whom I have known, steered the middle course. He never conceived that he had achieved a great success, but he never lost hope that by taking pains he might yet do so. Twelve years ago, when he was beginning to write that curious and fascinating book, *Prince Otto*, he wrote to me describing the mood in which one should go about one's work – golden words, which I have never forgotten. "One should strain," he said, "and then play, strain again, and play again. The strain is for us, it educates; the play is for the reader, and pleases. In moments of effort one learns to do the easy things that people like."

He learned that which he desired, and he gained more than he hoped for. He became the most exquisite English writer of his generation; yet those who lived close to him are apt to think less of this than of the fact that he was the most unselfish and the most lovable of human beings.

1895.

Christina Rossetti

1830–1894

This portrait of Christina Rossetti also comes from *Critical Kit-Kats* (1896). In his preface to that book Gosse explained his title, which came from the visual arts. "For the low comfortable rooms where people dined in the last century, there was invented the shorter and still less obtrusive picture called a Kit-Kat, and some of our most skilful painters have delighted in this modest form of portraiture, which emphasizes the head, yet does not quite exclude the hand of the sitter." The first version of Gosse's "Kit-Kat" of Christina Rossetti was written in 1882 and was undertaken at the suggestion of her brother, Dante Gabriel Rossetti, who told Gosse he had an appreciation of his sister such as was unusual at that time. Before it was published, Dante Gabriel died and Gosse put aside his piece "in the agitation produced by that event". Gosse knew Dante Gabriel far better than he knew Christina. When Hall Caine was preparing his *Recollections of D G Rossetti* in 1882, he told Gosse that Rossetti "constantly talked of you", and regretted that there was so little written evidence of their relationship. Even with that prompting, Gosse seems never to have written about Dante Gabriel. Eventually published in the *Century Magazine* in June 1893, there remains some evidence in the essay on Christina Rossetti that follows that she had helped with its composition.

* * *

So much has been written, since the untimely death of Dante Gabriel Rossetti, on the circumstances of his family history, that it is not requisite to enter very fully into that subject in the present sketch of his youngest sister. It is well known that the Italian poet Gabriele Rossetti, after a series of romantic adventures endured in the cause of liberty, settled in London, and married the

27

daughter of another Italian exile, G Polidori, Lord Byron's physician. From this stock, three-fourths of which was purely Italian, there sprang four children, of whom Dante Gabriel was the second, and Christina Georgina, born in December, 1830, the youngest. There was nothing in the training of these children which foreshadowed their various distinction in the future; although the transplanted blood ran quicker, no doubt, in veins that must now be called English, not Italian, even as the wine-red anemone broke into flower from the earth that was carried to the Campo Santo out of Palestine.

We cannot fathom these mysteries of transplantation. No doubt a thousand Italian families might settle in London, and their children be born as deaf to melody and as blind to Nature as their playfellows long native to Hoxton or Clerkenwell. Yet it is not possible to hold it quite an accident that this thousand and first family discovered in London soil the precise chemical qualities that made its Italian fibre break into clusters of blossom. Gabriel Rossetti, both as poet and painter, remained very Italian to the last, but his sister is a thorough Englishwoman. Unless I make a great mistake, she has scarcely visited Italy, and in her poetry the landscape and the observation of Nature are not only English, they are so thoroughly local that I doubt whether there is one touch in them all which proves her to have strayed more than fifty miles from London in any direction. I have no reason for saying so beyond internal evidence, but I should be inclined to suggest that the county of Sussex alone is capable of having supplied all the imagery which Miss Rossetti's poems contain. Her literary repertory, too, seems purely English; there is hardly a solitary touch in her work which betrays her transalpine parentage.

In a letter to myself, in words which she kindly lets me give to the public, Miss Rossetti has thus summed up some valuable impressions of her earliest bias toward writing:

"For me, as well as for Gabriel, whilst our 'school' was everything, it was no one definite thing. I, as the least and last of the group, may remind you that besides the clever and cultivated parents who headed us all, I in particular beheld far ahead of myself the clever sister and two clever brothers who were a little (though but a little) my seniors. And as to acquirements, I lagged out of all proportion behind them, and have never overtaken them to this day."

I interrupt my distinguished friend to remark that, even if we do not take this modest declaration with a grain of salt, it is interesting to find one more example of the fact that the possession of genius by no means presupposes a nature apt for what are called acquirements. Miss Rossetti proceeds:

"If any one thing schooled me in the direction of poetry, it was perhaps the delightful idle liberty to prowl all alone about my grandfather's cottage-grounds some thirty miles from London, entailing in my childhood a long stage-coach journey! This privilege came to an end when I was eight years old, if not earlier. The grounds were quite small, and on the simplest scale – but in those days to me they were vast, varied, worth exploring. After those charming holidays ended I remained pent up in London till I was a great girl of fourteen, when delight reawakened at the sight of primroses in a railway cutting – a prelude to many lovely country sights."

My impression is that a great deal of judicious neglect was practised in the Rossetti family, and that, like so many people of genius, the two poets, brother and sister, contrived to evade the educational mill. From the lips of Miss Christina herself I have it that all through her early girlhood she lay as a passive weight on the hands of those who invited her to explore those bosky groves called arithmetic, grammar, and the use of the globes. In Mr R L Stevenson's little masterpiece of casuistry called *On Idlers and Idling*, he has discussed the temper of mind so sympathetically that I will say no more than this, that Philistia never will comprehend the certain fact that, to genius, Chapter VI, which is primroses in a railway cutting, is often far more important than Chapter XIII, which happens to be the subjunctive mood. But for these mysteries of education I must refer the ingenuous reader to Mr Stevenson's delightful pages.

From her early childhood Miss Rossetti seems to have prepared herself for the occupation of her life, the art of poetry. When she was eleven her verses began to be noticed and preserved, and an extremely rare little volume, the very cynosure of Victorian bibliography, permits us to observe the development of her talent. One of the rarest of books – when it occasionally turns up at sales it commands an extravagant price – is *Verses by Christina G Rossetti*, privately printed in 1847, at the press of her grandfather Mr G Polidori, "at No. 15, Park Village East, Regent's Park, London." This little volume of sixty-six pages, dedicated to the author's mother, and preceded by a pretty little preface signed by Mr Polidori, is a curious revelation of the evolution of the poet's genius. There is hardly one piece in it which Miss Rossetti would choose to reprint in a collected edition of her works, but there are many which possess the greatest interest to a student of her mature style. The earliest verses – since all are dated – show us merely the child's desire for expression in verse, for experiment in rhyme and meter. Gradually we see the buddings of an individual manner, and in the latest piece, "The Dead City," the completion of which seems to have led to the printing of the little collection, we find the poet assuming something of her adult manner. [There] are some stanzas from this rarest of booklets, which will be new, in every probability, to all my readers, and in these we detect, unmistakably, the accents of the future author of *Goblin Market*. Three years later, in 1850, she was already a finished poet . . .

It was not my privilege to meet her more than some dozen times in the flesh, and those times mainly in the winter of 1870–71. But on most of those occasions I had the good fortune to converse with her for a long while; and up to a few months before her death we corresponded at not particularly distant intervals. She is known to the world, and very happily known, by her brother's portraits of her, and in particular by the singularly beautiful chalk drawing in profile, dated 1866. I think that tasteful arrangement of dress might have made her appear a noble and even a romantic figure so late as 1870, but, as I suppose, an ascetic or almost methodistical reserve caused her to clothe herself in a style, or with an absence of style, which was really distressing; her dark hair was streaked across her olive forehead, and turned up in a chignon; the high stiff dress ended in a hard collar and plain brooch, the extraordinarily ordinary skirt sank over a belated crinoline, and these were inflictions hard to bear from the high-priestess of Preraphaelitism. When it is added that her manner, from shyness, was of a portentous solemnity, that she had no small talk whatever, and that the common topics of the day appeared to be entirely unknown to her, it will be understood that she was considered highly formidable by the young and the flighty. I have seen her sitting alone, in the midst of a noisy drawing-room, like a pillar of cloud, a Sibyl whom no one had the audacity to approach.

Yet a kinder or simpler soul, or one less concentrated on self, or of a humbler sweetness, never existed. And to an enthusiast, who broke the bar of conventional chatter, and ventured on real subjects, her heart seemed to open like an unsealed fountain. The heavy lids of her weary-looking, bistred, Italian eyes would lift and display her ardour as she talked of the mysteries of poetry and religion. My visits to her, in her mother's house, 56 Euston Square, were abruptly brought to a close. On May 1, 1871, I received a note from her elder sister Maria warning me not to dine with them on the following Tuesday, as her sister was suddenly and alarmingly ill. This was, in fact, the mysterious complaint which thenceforth kept Christina bedridden, and sometimes at the point of death, for two years. She recovered, but the next time I saw her – she was well enough to be working in the British Museum in the summer of 1873 – she was so strangely altered as to be scarcely recognizable.

By degrees, to my great satisfaction, Miss Christina came to look upon me as in some little sense her champion in the press. "The pen you use for me has always a soft rather than a hard nib," she said, and in truth, whenever I found an opportunity of praising her pure and admirable poems, I was not slow to employ it. That I was not exempt, however, from an occasional peck even from this gentlest of turtle-doves, a letter (written in December 1875) reminds me. I had reviewed somewhere the first collected edition of her *Poems*, and I had ventured to make certain reservations. There are some points of valuable self-analysis which make a part of this letter proper to be quoted here:

'Save me from my friends! You are certainly up in your subject, and as I *might* have fared worse in other hands I will not regret that rival reviewer [Mr Theodore Watts] who was hindered from saying his say. As to the lamented early lyrics, I do not suppose myself to be the person least tenderly reminiscent of them [I had grumbled at the excision of some admirable favourites]; but it at any rate appears to be the commoner fault amongst verse-writers to write what is not worth writing, than to suppress what would merit hearers. I for my part am a great believer in the genuine poetic impulse belonging (very often) to the spring and not to the autumn of life, and some established reputations fail to shake me in this opinion; at any rate, if so one feels the possibility to stand in one's own case, then I vote that the grace of silence succeed the grace of song. By all which I do not bind myself to unbroken silence, but meanwhile I defend my position – or, you may retort, I do not defend it. By-the-by, your *upness* does not prevent my protesting that Edith and Maggie did not dream or even nap; *Flora* did; but have I not caught *you* napping? Do, pray, come and see me and we will not fight."

It is difficult to speak of either of the Rossetti ladies without a reference to the elder sister, whom also I had the privilege of knowing in early days. She left upon me the impression of stronger character, though of narrower intellect and infinitely poorer imagination. I formed the idea, I know not whether with justice, that the pronounced high-church views of Maria, who throve on ritual, starved the less pietistic, but painfully conscientious nature of Christina. The influence of Maria Francesca Rossetti on her sister seemed to be like that of Newton upon Cowper, a species of police surveillance exercised by a hard, convinced mind over a softer and more fanciful one. Miss Maria Rossetti, who generally needed the name of Dante to awaken her from a certain social torpor, died in 1876, but not until she had set her seal on the religious habits of her sister. Such, at least, was the notion which I formed, perhaps on slight premises.

That the conscience of the younger sister was, in middle life, so tender as to appear almost morbid, no one, I think, will deny. I recall an amusing instance of it. In the winter of 1874, I was asked to secure some influential signatures to a petition against the destruction of a part of the New Forest. Mr Swinburne promised me his, if I could induce Miss Christina Rossetti to give hers, suggesting as he did so, that the feat might not be an easy one. In fact, I found that no little palaver was necessary; but at last she was so far persuaded of the innocence of the protest that she wrote *Chr*; she then stopped, dropped the pen, and said very earnestly, "Are you sure that they do not propose to build churches on the land?" After a long time, I succeeded in convincing her that such a scheme was not thought of, and she proceeded to write *istina G Ros*, and stopped again. "Nor school-houses?" fluctuating with tremulous scruple. At length she finished the signature, and I carried the parchment off to claim the fulfilment of Mr Swinburne's promise. And the labourer felt that he was worthy of his hire.

On the 6th of July, 1876, I saw Christina Rossetti for the last time. I suppose that her life, during the last twenty years of it, was as sequestered as that of any pious woman in a religious house. She stirred but little, I fancy, from her rooms save to attend the services of the Anglican church. That her mind continued humane and simple her successive publications and her kind and sometimes playful letters proved. Misfortunes attended her family, and she who had been the centre of so eager and vivid a group, lived to find herself almost solitary. At length, on the 29th of December, 1894, after prolonged sufferings borne with infinite patience, this great writer, who was also a great saint, passed into the region of her visions.

1882–1896.

Richard Hengist Horne

1802–1884

This essay on Horne comes from *Portraits and Sketches*, the collection Gosse published in 1912. It appeared first in the *North American Review* for April, 1899. In his preface to the volume, Gosse called Horne "a typical product" of "the transitional period between Shelley and Keats on the one hand and Tennyson and Browning on the other". He bracketed Horne with Philip Bailey, the author of *Festus*, and said "those who had an opportunity of conversing with these interesting and pathetic figures in their old age are growing rare, while no life of either of them has appeared." Rather surprisingly perhaps (as his poetry is almost entirely forgotten) a full-scale biography of Horne called *The Farthing Poet* – for reasons Gosse's essay will make clear – appeared in 1968. Its author, Ann Blainey, was born in Castlemaine in the centre of the Australian goldfields where Horne had worked in the 1850s. The justification for the biography is also the justification for including Gosse's essay on Horne in this collection. His was such an odd life.

* * *

The publication of the love letters which passed, in 1845 and 1846, between Robert Browning and Elizabeth Barrett blew a little of the dust off several names which were brightly before the public then and have become sadly obscured since . . . Amongst the names, faintly echoing from the earliest Victorian period, we meet with one more than the rest deserving of perpetuation, with at all events a greater mass of actually accomplished work attached to it, the name of Mr Horne, the author of "Cosmo de Medici," of "Gregory VII," and, above all, of "the farthing epic," the once extremely celebrated "Orion." And with this there comes vividly back to me a vision of an extraordinary personage, of whom I saw a great deal in my youth, and of whom I feel disposed to garner some of my impressions before I lose them.

He had been baptized Richard Henry Horne, but in late middle life he had changed the second of these names to Hengist. It was in 1874 that I set eyes on him first, in circumstances which were somewhat remarkable. The occasion was the marriage of the poet, Arthur O'Shaughnessy, to the eldest daughter of Westland Marston, the playwright. There was a large and distinguished company present, and most of the prominent "Pre-Raphaelites," as they were still occasionally called. In the midst of the subsequent festivities, and when the bride was surrounded by her friends, a tiny old gentleman cleared a space around him, and, all uninvited, began to sit upon the floor and sing, in a funny little cracked voice, Spanish songs to his own accompaniment on the guitar. He was very unusual in appearance. Although he was quite bald at the top of his head, his milk-white hair was luxuriant at the sides, and hung in clusters of ringlets. His moustache was so long that it became whisker, and in that condition drooped, also in creamy ringlets, below his chin. The elder guests were inclined to be impatient, the younger to ridicule this rather tactless interruption. Just as it seemed possible something awkward would happen, Robert Browning stepped up and said, in his loud, cheerful voice: "That was charming, Horne! It quite took us to 'the warm South' again," and cleverly leading the old gentleman's thoughts to a different topic, he put an end to the incident.

This scene was very characteristic of Horne, who was gay, tactless, and vain to a remarkable degree. He had lately come back from Australia, where nothing had gone well with him for long together, and he did not understand the ways of the younger generation in London. But to those who could be patient with his peculiarities he offered a very amusing study. He had delightful stories, many of which are still inedited, of the great men of his youth – Wordsworth, Hunt, Hazlitt, in particular. But he himself, with his incredible mixture of affectation and fierceness, humour and absurdity, enthusiasm and ignorance, with his incoherency of appearance, at once so effeminate and so muscular, was better than all his tales. He was a combination of the troubadour and the prize-fighter, on a miniature scale. It was impossible not to think of a curly white poodle when one looked at him, especially when he would throw his fat little person on a sofa and roll about, with gestures less dignified than were, perhaps, ever before seen in a poet of between seventy and eighty years of age. And yet he had a fine, buoyant spirit, and a generous imagination with it all. But the oddity of it, alas! is what lingers in the memory – those milky ringlets, that extraordinary turn of the head, that embrace of the beribboned guitar!

In a pathetic little letter which Horne wrote to me in his eightieth year, he said, quite placidly, that though he was now forgotten, no poet had ever had more pleasant things said of him by people dead and gone. It was perfectly true. Wordsworth and Tennyson, Leigh Hunt and Walter Savage Landor, had all praised his poetry; Carlyle had declared that "the fire of the stars was in him," and G. H. Lewes that he was "a man of the most unquestionable genius." How highly Robert and Elizabeth Browning regarded him may be seen over and over again in the course of their correspondence. But his talent was of a very fugitive kind. He was a remarkable poet for seven or eight years, and a tiresome and uninspired scribbler for the rest of his life. His period of good work began in 1837, when he published "Cosmo de Medici" and "The Death of Marlowe"; it closed in 1843, with the publication of "Orion," and the composition of all that was best in the "Ballad Romances." If any one wished to do honour to the *manes* of poor old Horne – and in these days far less distinguished poets than he receive the honours of rediscovery – the way to do it would be to publish in one volume the very best of his writings, and nothing more. The badness of the bulk of his later verse is outside all calculation. How a man who had once written so well as he, could ever come to write, for instance, "Bible Tragedies" (1881) is beyond all skill of the literary historian to comprehend.

But, although Horne was, for a short time, a good poet, he was always more interesting as a human being. His whole life was an adventure; it was like a "book for boys." He was pleased to relate that even his birth was not ordinary, for he came into the world so exactly at the stroke of midnight on the last day of the year that it could never be decided whether he was born in 1802 or 1803. I do not know who his parents were or what his family. In the days when I saw so much of him he appeared to be quite solitary; he never spoke of possessing a relative. He was trained for the army, and lost his chance through some foolish escapade. But before this he had been at school at Enfield, where Tom Keats, the poet's brother, and Charles Wells, who wrote "Joseph and his Brethren," had been his school-fellows. He used to tell us in his old age that he was once scampering out of school, when he saw the chaise of Mr Hammond, the surgeon, standing at the door. John Keats, who was Hammond's apprentice, was holding the horse, his head sunken forward in a brown study; the boys, who knew how pugnacious Keats was, dared Horne to throw a snowball at him, which Horne did, hitting Keats in the back of the head and then escaping round the corner at a headlong pace. It used to be very thrilling, in the eighties, to hear the old gentleman tell how he had actually snowballed Keats; almost as though one should arise and say that he had sold Shakespeare a cheesecake.

Just before he should have entered Sandhurst the young Horne was lured away to America, and offered himself as a volunteer in the War of Mexican Independence. He entered the new Mexican navy as a midshipman, and dashed about under irregular fire at the bombardment of Vera Cruz and at the siege of San Juan Ulloa. He used to tell us that he never would miss his swim in the sea in the morning, nor return to the ship until he had been well within range of the guns of Vera Cruz. The Spaniards could never hit him, he said; but one day when he was making a long nose at the gunners, he was as nearly as possible swallowed from behind by a shark. I forget how he accounted for his escape, but there was always a good deal of Baron Munchausen about Mr Horne.

When the Mexican War was over, he strolled across the United States, with a belt full of doubloons girded about his person, and visited the Mohawks, the Oneidas, and the Hurons. He had a fight with a Red Indian brave and beat him, and carried away a bunch of eagle-feathers from his body. After many strange adventures, he must needs bathe in public under the cataract of Niagara. Two of his ribs were found to be broken when he was fished out again, insensible. He then took a steerage passage in a steamer that was wrecked in the St Lawrence. He walked in moccasins over to Halifax, Nova Scotia, and started again in a timber ship, whose crew rose in mutiny and set fire to her in mid-Atlantic; Mr Horne quelled the mutiny and put out the fire, to the eternal gratitude of the captain, who fell upon his knees upon the deck and kissed his hands. I delighted in Mr Horne's stories of his past life, but sometimes I used to fear that he exaggerated.

It was not until he was thirty years of age that Horne began to take up literature, and he was thirty-five when he enjoyed his first success with "Cosmo de Medici," an historical tragedy in blank verse, which has some very fine passages, and was greatly admired in the London coteries. Then came the period of seven years, of which I have spoken, in which Horne really took his place, with Browning and Tennyson, as one of the promising poets of the age. If he had died in 1844, he would probably hold a high place still, as an "inheritor of unfulfilled renown," but unfortunately he lived for forty more years, and never discovered that his talent had abandoned him. His "Orion," which was published in 1843, was brought out at the price of one farthing. Elizabeth Barrett sent out to the nearest bookshop for a shilling's worth, but was refused her four dozen copies. Purchasers had to produce their brass farthing for each "Orion," and no change was given. This was done "to mark the public contempt into which epic poetry has fallen," but it was also a very good advertisement. Everybody talked about Mr Horne's "farthing" poem, and after some editions had run out the price was cautiously raised. But when the tenth edition appeared, at a cost of seven shillings, the public perceived that its leg was being pulled, and it purchased "Orion" no more. In spite of all this, "Orion" is far indeed from being a humorous composition; it is a dignified and melodious romance of Greek symbolism, with some remote relation to the "Hyperion" of Keats, and contains some admirable passages . . .

It is known to Apollo only what varied employments Horne took up when the Muses began to abandon him. He was sub-editor of *Household Words* under Dickens, and special commissioner of the *Daily News* to Ireland when the great famine broke out. Suddenly, and desperately determined to marry, he went down to stay with Miss Mitford in Berkshire, and proposed to all the neighbouring heiresses one after another, to the intense indignation of that lady, who declared that he had used her hospitable dining-room, on the same day, to propose to a lady (with £50,000 a year) at lunch, and to another (with £40,000 a year) at tea. None of these efforts was crowned with success; perhaps he had the presumption to be in love with Elizabeth Barrett, whom he had at that time never seen, although oceans of correspondence had passed between them. At all events, directly Robert Browning had carried off his eminent bride, Horne appeared with a little Miss Foggs upon his arm, whom he presently married. They did not get on together; why should history conceal the fact, when Horne himself was wont to dilate upon it so freely to his friends? Mrs Horne, in tears, threw herself upon the paternal sympathy of Charles Dickens, and Horne indignantly sought a southern hemisphere.

In Australia he was commander of the Gold Escort, and it was delightful, years afterwards, to hear him tell how he convoyed several tons of bullion from Ballarat to Melbourne amid every circumstance of peril. Then he became Gold Commissioner to the

Government, but here his flow of high spirits carried him away. He then flung himself into the cultivation of the cochineal insect, edited a Victorian newspaper, became Commissioner of Waterworks, gave lessons in gymnastics, professed the art of natation, and was one of the starters of Australian wine-growing. Long afterwards, when the first Australian cricketers came over to England, Horne wrote to me: "I learn that the cricketers have made *each* £1000 over here! Why, oh! why did not I become an Australian cricketer, instead of an unprofitable swimmer? When years no longer smiled upon my balls and runs, I might have retired upon my laurelled bat, and have published tragedies at my own expense. Is there any redress for these things in another world? I don't think so; I shall be told I had my choice." He certainly paid his money. No one, I suppose, ever failed in so many brilliant, unusual enterprises, every one of which was sure to succeed when he adopted it.

When he came back from Australia, I think about 1869, he was in very low water. He had managed very deeply to offend Charles Dickens, who had taken up the cause of Horne's neglected wife. What happened to Horne in the early years after his return I never heard; I fancy that he went abroad again for some part of the time. A little later Robert Browning, who had always felt a sincere regard for Horne, was able to be of practical service to him. He was encouraged to republish his poems, and to appeal by means of them to the new age. In these days one used to meet him at afternoon parties, carrying with great care, under his arm, the precious guitar, which he called "my daughter," and was used ceremoniously to introduce as "Miss Horne." A little later in the evening Horne would be discovered on a low stool, warbling Mexican romances, or murmuring with exaggerated gallantry to the prettiest girl in the room. All this time he was thirsting for publicity – if he could only be engaged to sing in public, to box in public, to swim in public, how happy he would be! It used to be said that when he was nearly seventy, Horne persuaded the captain of a ship to tie his legs together and fling him into the sea, and that he swam with ease to the boat. A wonderful little ringleted athlete, no doubt!

A great deal of Horne's work in verse, and even in prose, remains unpublished, and is not very likely, I should think, to be ever printed. As I have said, his faculty, which had been so graceful, faded away from him about forty years before he died. When he

was in Australia he wrote a good deal, among other things a
choral drama, "Prometheus, the Fire-Bringer," which was actually
composed out in the bush, and lost, and written all over again,
still in the bush. The first edition of this poem is styled "by
Richard *Henry* Horne," and the second, which followed soon
after, "by Richard *Hengist* Horne," showing the period at which
he adopted the more barbaric name . . .

Horne's cheerfulness was a very pleasant feature in his character.
Life had treated him scurvily, love had missed him, fame had
come down and crowned him, and then had rudely snatched the
laurel away. If ever a man might have been excused for sourness,
it was Horne. But he was a gallant little old man, and if it was
impossible not to smile at him, it was still less possible not to
recognize his courage and his spirit. Curiously enough, Elizabeth
Barrett, who carried on so close a correspondence with Horne in
her unmarried days, but who, warned by Miss Mitford, never
would allow him to call upon her in person, had an accurate
instinct of his merits and his weaknesses, and all the casual
remarks about Horne which she makes in the course of her letters
to Robert Browning strike one who knew Horne well in later
years as singularly exact and perspicacious. His edition of her
letters to him, published about twenty years ago in two volumes,
is becoming a rare book, and contains many things of remarkable
interest and importance.

It was from 1876 to 1879 that we saw him most frequently. He
was living at this time in two rooms in Northumberland Street,
Regent's Park, in very great poverty, which he bore with the
gayest and most gallant *insouciance*. An attempt was made –
indeed, several attempts were made – to secure for him a little
pension from the Civil List, and these were supported by Carlyle
and Browning, Tennyson and Swinburne, to name no smaller fry.
But all in vain; for some reason, absolutely inscrutable to me,
these efforts were of no avail. It was darkly said that there were
reasons why Mr Gladstone would never, never yield; and he never
did. When Lord Beaconsfield came into office, he granted the
poor little old man £50 a year, but even then he had not too much
food to eat nor clothes to keep him warm. Still he went bravely
on, shaking his white ringlets and consoling himself with his guitar.
He was fond of mystery, which is a great consoler. For economy's
sake, he used to write on post-cards, but always with a great deal
of care, so that the postman should be none the wiser. I have

such a post-card before me now; it is an answer to a proposal of mine that he should come in and take dinner with us:

Nov. 29, 1877.

The Sharpshooter's friendly shot just received. By adroitly porting my helm, and hauling out my flying jib, I shall, by 7 o'clock this evening, be able to get the weather-gauge of the Cape I was bound for, and run into your Terrace. Thine,

REEFER

Nothing, surely, could be more discreet than that.

To the very last he was anxious to regain his old place as a man of letters, and his persistency was really quite pathetic. One did not know what to do with his suggestions. I appeal to any one acquainted with the business of literature whether anything can be more trying than to receive this sort of communication:

"Don't you think curiosity might be aroused if you could induce the editor of the ——— to print something of this kind: 'We understand that a leading periodical will shortly contain a Dramatic Scene by the Author of 'Orion,' entitled 'The Circle of the Regicides,' in which such interlocutors as Dr Kobold, Prof Franz Tollkopf, Hans Arbeitsdulder, and Baron Dumm von Ehrsucht will represent certain well-known characters. There will also be brought upon the scene the Apparitions of Brutus, Cromwell, the patriot Mazzini, and the philanthropist Robert Owen; together with a chorus of French and Russian revolutionists, with a trio and chorus of female Regicides.' On second thoughts, perhaps, better stop after 'Owen.'"

It was difficult to bring such suggestions as these within the range of practical literature.

Horne's physical strength was very extraordinary in old age. It was strangely incompatible with the appearance of the little man, with his ringleted locks and mincing ways. But he was past seventy before he ceased to challenge powerful young swimmers to feats of natation, and he very often beat them, carrying off from them cups and medals, to their deep disgust. He was nearly eighty when he filled us, one evening, with alarm by bending our drawing-room poker to an angle in striking it upon the strained muscles

40

of his fore-arm. He was very vain of his physical accomplishments, and he used to declare that he was in training to be a centenarian. These are things that should never be said, they tempt the fates; so one day, just after poor Mr Horne had been boasting, he was knocked down by a van in Lisson Grove, and, although he rallied in a wonderful way, he was never the same man again. Presently, on March 13, 1884, he died at Margate, whither he had been removed to take the benefit of the sea-air. He was in his eighty-second year. It would be a great pity that a man so unique and so picturesque should be forgotten. As long as the world is interested in Elizabeth Barrett Browning, Horne can never be entirely forgotten, but he deserves to be remembered for his own sake.

1899.

Robert Browning

1812–1889

From the way Gosse mentions Browning at Arthur O'Shaughnessy's wedding (as described in the preceding essay), it would seem he already knew him then. Ten years later, when Gosse was applying for the Clark Lectureship at Cambridge, they knew each other well. Browning wrote to the Rev. J D Williams: "My friend Gosse is a candidate for this new Professorship of Literature at Cambridge. He is an exceedingly fit man for the post, I think – as men now go and are in evidence. Tennyson thinks the same." Browning and Gosse had become near-neighbours in 1876 when the Gosses took a house in Delamere Terrace, a continuation of Warwick Crescent where Browning lived. Gosse would often call in ("on my way down in the morning") when Browning was in England.

The essay printed here forms the last section, "Personal Impressions", of Gosse's small book on Browning: *Robert Browning: Personalia*. My copy, bound in white vellum, carries the imprint of Houghton, Mifflin and Company of Boston and New York and the date 1890. In the Preface Gosse writes that most of the book originally appeared in *The Century Magazine* of December 1881. This part, "The Early Career of Robert Browning", "was inspired and partly dictated, was revised and was approved of, by himself". Browning had been so irritated by the latest of a series of accounts of his life ("mainly fabulous") that he had decided to put the record straight with Gosse's help. Reprinting this *Century* article in 1890, Gosse added to it "some slight recollections of the personal characteristics" of his friend, which first appeared in the *New Review* for January 1890, and it is these recollections that follow. He ended his Preface to the book:

If such notes as these are to have any permanent value, they must be recorded before the imagination has had time to play tricks with the memory. Such as they are, I am sure they are faithful today; tomorrow I should be sure of nothing.

* * *

43

Those who have frequently seen our revered and beloved friend during the past year will hardly join in the general chorus of surprise which has greeted the death of one so strong in appearance and so hale and green. Rather with these there will be a faint sort of congratulation that such a life, so manifestly waning in essential vigor, should have been spared the indignities of decline, the "cold gradations of decay." For a year past no close observer could have doubted that the robustness which seemed still invincible in the summer of 1888 was rudely shaken. Cold upon cold left the poet weaker; the recuperative power was rapidly and continuously on the decrease. But a little while ago, and to think of Mr Browning and of illness together seemed impossible. It is a singular fact that he who felt so keenly for human suffering had scarcely known, by experience, what physical pain was. The vigor, the exemption from feebleness, which marks his literary genius, accompanied the man as well. I recollect his giving a picturesque account of a headache he suffered from, once, in St Petersburg, about the year 1834! Who amongst us is fortunate enough to remember his individual headaches? I seem to see him now, about six years ago, standing in the east wind on the doorstep of his house in Warwick Crescent, declaring with emphasis that he felt ill, really ill, more ill than he had felt for half a century, and looking all the while, in spite of that indisposition, a monument of sturdy health. Even his decline has been the reluctant fall of a wholesome and well-balanced being. Painlessly, without intellectual obscuration, demanding none of that pity that he deprecated, he falls asleep in Italy, faint indeed, yet, to the very last, pursuing. Since those we love must pass away; since the light must sooner or later sink in the lantern, there is, perhaps, no better way than this . . .

It is natural in these first moments to think more of the man than of his works. The latter remain with us, and coming generations will comprehend them better than we do. But our memories of the former, though far less salient, have this importance – that they will pass away with us. Every hour henceforward makes the man more shadowy. We must condense our recollections, if they are not to prove wholly volatile and fugitive. In these few pages, then, I shall mainly strive to contribute my pencil-sketch to the gallery of portraits which will be preserved. He was so many-sided that there may be room for any picture of him that is quite sincere and personal, however slight it may prove; and in the case of Mr Browning, far more than of most men of genius, the portrait may be truly and boldly drawn without offense. There is no prominent feature of character which has to be slurred over, no trick or foible to be concealed. No man ever showed a more handsome face to private friendship, no one disappointed or repelled less, no one, upon intimate acquaintance, required less to be apologized for or explained away.

There have been many attempts to describe Mr Browning as a talker in society . . . But his private conversation was a very different thing from his talk over the dinner-table or in a picture-gallery. It was a very much finer phenomenon, and one which tallied far better with the noble breadth of his genius. To a single listener, with whom he was on familiar terms, the Browning of his own study was to the Browning of a dinner party as a tiger is to a domestic cat. In such conversation his natural strength came out. His talk assumed the volume and the tumult of a cascade. His voice rose to a shout, sank to a whisper, ran up and down the gamut of conversational melody. Those whom he was expecting will never forget his welcome, the loud trumpet-note from the other end of the passage, the talk already in full flood at a distance of twenty feet. Then, in his own study or drawing-room, what he loved was to capture the visitor in a low armchair's "sofa-lap of leather," and from a most unfair vantage of height to tyrannize, to walk around the victim, in front, behind, on this side, on that, weaving magic circles, now with gesticulating arms thrown high, now grovelling on the floor to find some reference in a folio, talking all the while, a redundant turmoil of thoughts, fancies, and reminiscences flowing from those generous lips. To think of it is to conjure up an image of intellectual vigor, armed at every point, but overflowing, none the less, with the geniality of strength.

The last time that the present writer enjoyed one of these never-to-be-forgotten talks was on the earliest Sunday in June last summer. For the first time since many years Mr Browning was in Cambridge, and he was much fêted. He proposed a temporary retreat from too full society, and we retired alone to the most central and sequestered part of the beautiful Fellows' Garden of Trinity. A little tired and silent at first, he was no sooner well ensconced under the shadow of a tree, in a garden-chair, than his tongue became unloosed. The blue sky was cloudless above, summer foliage hemmed us round in a green mist, a pink mountain of a double-may in blossom rose in front. We were close to a hot shrub of sweetbriar that exhaled its balm in the sunshine. Commonly given to much gesticulation, the poet sat quite still on this occasion; and, the perfect quiet being only broken by his voice, the birds lost fear and came closer and closer, curiously peeping. So we sat for more than two hours, and I could but note what I had had opportunity to note before, that although, on occasion, he could be so accurate an observer of nature, it was not instinctive with him to observe. In the blaze of summer, with all the life of birds and insects moving around us, he did not borrow an image from or direct an allusion to any natural fact about us.

He sat and talked of his own early life and aspirations; how he marvelled, as he looked back, at the audacious obstinacy which had made him, when a youth, determine to be a poet and nothing but a poet. He remarked that all his life long he had never known what it was to have to do a certain thing to-day and not to-morrow; he thought this had led to superabundance of production, since, on looking back, he could see that he had often, in his unfettered leisure, been afraid to do nothing. Then, with complete frankness, he described the long-drawn desolateness of his early and middle life as a literary man; how, after certain spirits had seemed to rejoice in his first sprightly runnings, and especially in *Paracelsus*, a blight had fallen upon his very admirers. He touched, with a slight irony, on "the entirely unintelligible *Sordello*," and the forlorn hope of *Bells and Pomegranates*. Then he fell, more in the habitual manner of old men, to stories of early loves and hatreds, Italian memories of the forties, stories with names in them that meant nothing to his ignorant listener. And, in the midst of these reminiscences, a chord of extreme interest to the critic was touched. For in recounting a story of some Tuscan nobleman who had shown him two exquisite miniature paintings, the work of a young artist who should have received for them the prize in some local contest, and who, being unjustly defrauded, broke his ivories, burned his brushes, and indignantly forswore the thankless art for ever, Mr Browning suddenly reflected that there was, as he said, "stuff for a poem" in that story, and immediately with extreme vivacity began to sketch the form it should take, the suppression of what features and the substitution of what others were needful; and finally suggested the non-obvious or inverted moral of the whole, in which the act of spirited defiance was shown to be, really, an act of tame renunciation, the poverty of the artist's spirit being proved in his eagerness to snatch, even though it was by honest merit, a benefit simply material. The poet said, distinctly, that he had never before reflected on this incident as one proper to be versified; the speed, therefore, with which the creative architect laid the foundations, built the main fabric, and even put on the domes and pinnacles

46

of his poem was, no doubt, of uncommon interest. He left it, in five minutes, needing nothing but the mere outward crust of the versification. It will be a matter of some curiosity to see whether the poem so started and sketched was actually brought to completion.

It cannot have escaped the notice of any one who knew Robert Browning well, and who compares him in thought with other men of genius whom he may have known, that it was not his strength only, his vehement and ever-eruptive force, that distinguished him, but to an almost equal extent his humanity. Of all great poets, except (one fancies) Chaucer, he must have been the most accessible. It is almost a necessity with imaginative genius of a very high order to require support from without: sympathy, admiration, amusement, must be constantly poured in to balance the creative evaporation. But Mr Browning demanded no such tribute. He rather hastened forward with both hands full of entertainment for the new-comer, anxious to please rather than hoping to be pleased. The most part of men of genius look upon an unknown comer as certainly a bore and probably an enemy, but to Robert Browning the whole world was full of vague possibilities of friendship. No one resented more keenly an unpleasant specimen of humanity, no one could snub more royally at need, no one was – certain premises being established – more ruthless in administering the *coup de grâce*; but then his surprise gave weight to his indignation. He had assumed a new acquaintance to be a good fellow, and behold! against all ordinary experience, he had turned out to be a bore or a sneak. Sudden, irreparable chastisement must fall on one who had proved the poet's optimism to be at fault. And, to those who shared a nearer intimacy than genial acquaintanceship could offer, is there one left to-day who was disappointed in his Browning or had any deep fault to find with him as a friend? Surely, no! He was human to the core, red with the warm blood to the centre of his being; and if he erred, as he occasionally did – as lately, to the sorrow of all who knew him, he did err – it was the judgment not the instinct that was amiss. He was a poet, after all, and not a philosopher.

It was part of Mr Browning's large optimism, of his splendid and self-sufficing physical temperament, that he took his acquaintances easily – it might almost be said superficially. His poetic creations crowded out the real world to a serious extent. With regard to living men and women he was content to speculate, but with the children of his brain the case was different. These were not the subjects of more or less indolent conjecture, but of absolute knowl-

47

edge. It must be ten years ago, but the impression of the incident is as fresh upon me as though it happened yesterday, that Mr Browning passed from languid and rather ineffectual discussion of some persons well known to us both into vivid and passionate apology for an act of his own Colombe of Ravenstein. It was the flash from conventionality to truth, from talk about people whom he hardly seemed to see to a record of a soul that he had formed and could follow through all the mazes of caprice. It was seldom, even in intimacy, I think, that he would talk thus liberally about his sons and daughters of the pen, but that was mainly from a sensible reticence and hatred of common vanity. But when he could be induced to discuss his creations, it was easy to see how vividly the whole throng of them was moving in the hollow of his mind. It is doubtful whether he ever totally forgot any one of the vast assemblage of his characters.

In this close of our troubled century, . . . the robust health of Robert Browning's mind and body has presented a singular and a most encouraging phenomenon. He missed the morbid over-refinement of the age; the processes of his mind were sometimes even a little coarse, and always delightfully direct. For real delicacy he had full appreciation, but he was brutally scornful of all exquisite morbidness. The vibration of his loud voice, his hard fist upon the table, would make very short work with cobwebs. But this external roughness, like the rind of a fruit, merely served to keep the inner sensibilities young and fresh. None of his instincts grew old. Long as he lived, he did not live long enough for one of his ideals to vanish, for one of his enthusiasms to lose its heat; to the last, as he so truly said, he "never doubted clouds would break, Never dreamed, though right were worsted, wrong would triumph." The subtlest of writers, he was the simplest of men, and he learned in serenity what he taught in song.

1889.

Alfred Tennyson
1809–1892

In the absence of a full portrait of Tennyson, I am including two short essays and an extract from another. The first, remembering Gosse's own warning quoted on p. 43, may be inaccurate, written as it was 40 years after the meeting. It was published by Gosse in *Portraits and Sketches* (1912). If Browning was one of the writers of whom Gosse wrote after "the patient scrutiny of many years", the personal observations in the Tennyson pieces are "the result of a few flashing glimpses". These phrases come from Gosse's preface to the 1912 collection. The second essay, to which Gosse gave the title *Tennyson – and After*, appeared in *Questions at Issue* (1893). It is as much critical as biographical and Gosse, in his preface to the volume, is modest in his claims. "In speaking of what is proceeding around us no one can be trusted to be authoritative. The wisest, clearest and most experienced of critics have notoriously been wrong about the phenomena of their own day."

Some years later Gosse reviewed – or ruminated on – Strachey's *Eminent Victorians* and made some interesting remarks on the appendix of "Impressions", by a series of elderly friends, which closes the official *Life of Tennyson*, published in 1897. Gosse's piece appeared in the *Edinburgh Review* for October 1918, at a time when Tennyson's reputation was still in eclipse. My Tennyson section closes with a brief extract from this essay, which was reprinted in *Some Diversions of a Man of Letters* (1919) under the title "The Agony of the Victorian Age."

*   *   *

A FIRST SIGHT

There is a reaction in the popular feeling about Tennyson, and I am told that upon the young he has lost his hold, which was like that of an octopus upon us in my salad days. These revolutions in taste do not trouble me much; they are inevitable and they are not final. But those who "cannot read" "Maud" and "In Memoriam" to-day must take it on the word of a veteran that forty years ago we, equally, could not help reading them. There was a revolt against the tyranny now and then; in particular, after "The Loves of the Wrens" and "Enoch Arden" a rather serious mutiny broke out among Tennyson's admirers, but "Lucretius" appeared and they were enslaved again.

It is strange to look back upon the unrestrained panegyric which took the place of the higher criticism of Tennyson in the closing years of the nineteenth century. When a very clever man like the late Duke of Argyll, a man of sober years, could say, without being reproached, that Tennyson's blank verse in the "Idylls" was sweeter and stronger than "the stately march of Elizabethan English in its golden prime"; when Mr Gladstone could declare of Arthur in the same "Idylls" that he "knew not where to look in history or letters for a nobler or more overpowering conception of man as he might be," then a reaction, however tenderly delayed, was inevitable. The uncritical note of praise is almost more surely hurtful to a reputation than the uncritical note of blame, for it makes a wound that is much harder to heal. Tennyson is now suffering from the extravagant obsequiousness of his late Victorian admirers. At the moment of which I am about to speak, Tennyson had published nothing since "The Holy Grail," and it was understood that he was slightly startled by the arrival of Swinburne, Morris, and the Rossettis on a stage which he, with Robert Browning still very much in the background, had hitherto sufficiently filled. But the vogue of these new-comers was confined to the elect. In the world at large Tennyson was the English living poet *par excellence*, great by land and great by sea, the one survivor of the heroic chain of masters.

It was the early summer of 1871, and I was palely baking, like a crumpet, in a singularly horrible underground cage, made of steel bars, called the Den. This was a place such as no responsible being is allowed to live in nowadays, where the transcribers on the British Museum staff were immured in a half-light. This cellar was prominently brought forward a year or two later in the course of a Royal Commission on the British Museum, being "lifted into notice" only to be absolutely condemned by the indignation of the medical faculty. I was dolefully engaged here, being then one of the humblest of mankind, a Junior Assistant in the Printed Books Department of the British Museum, on some squalid task, in what was afterwards described by a witness as an atmosphere "scented with rotten morocco, and an indescribable odour familiar in foreign barracks," when a Senior Assistant, one of the rare just spirits in that academical Dotheboys Hall, W R S Ralston, came dashing down the flights of curling steel staircase, to the danger of his six feet six of height, and of the beard that waved down to his waist. Over me he bent, and in a whisper (we were forbidden to speak out loud in the Den) he said, "Come up stairs at once and be presented to Mr Tennyson!"

Proud young spirits of the present day, for whom life opens in adulation, will find it scarcely possible to realize what such a summons meant to me. As we climbed those steep and spiral staircases towards light and day, my heart pounded in my chest with agitation. The feeling of excitement was almost overwhelming: it was not peculiar to myself; such ardours were common in those years. Some day a philosopher must analyse it – that enthusiasm of the seventies, that intoxicating belief in "the might of poesy." Tennyson was scarcely a human being to us, he was the God of the Golden Bow; I approached him now like a blank idiot about to be slain, "or was I a worm, too low-crawling for death, O Delphic Apollo?" It is not merely that no person living now calls forth that kind of devotion, but the sentiment of mystery has disappeared. Not genius itself could survive the kodak snapshots and the halfpenny newspapers.

It must, I suppose, have been one of those days on which the public was then excluded, since we found Tennyson, with a single companion, alone in what was then the long First Sculpture Gallery. His friend was James Spedding, at whom in other conditions I should have gazed with interest, but in the Delphic presence he was not visible to my dazzled eyes. Mr Thornycroft's statue of the poet, now placed in Trinity College, gives an admirable impression of him at a slightly later date than 1871, if (that is) it is translated out of terms of white into terms of black. Tennyson, at that time, was still one of the darkest of men, as he is familiarly seen in all his earlier portraits. But those portraits do not give, although Mr Thornycroft has suggested, the singular majesty of his figure, standing in repose. Ralston, for all his six feet six, seemed to dwindle before this magnificent presence, while Tennyson stood, bare-headed among the Roman Emperors, every inch as imperial-

51

looking as the best of them. He stood there as we approached him, very still, with slightly drooping eyelids, and made no movement, no gesture of approach. When I had been presented, and had shaken his hand, he continued to consider me in a silence which would have been deeply disconcerting if it had not, somehow, seemed kindly, and even, absurd as it sounds, rather shy.

The stillness was broken by Ralston's irrelevantly mentioning that I was presently to start for Norway. The bard then began to talk about that country, which I was surprised to find he had visited some dozen years before. Ralston kindly engaged Spedding in conversation, so that Tennyson might now apply himself to me; with infinite goodness he did so, even "making conversation," for I was hopelessly tongue-tied, and must, in fact, have cut a very poor figure. Tennyson, it miraculously appeared, had read some of my stammering verses, and was vaguely gracious about them. He seemed to accept me as a sheep in the fold of which he was, so magnificently, the shepherd. This completed my undoing, but he did not demand from me speech. He returned to the subject of Norway, and said it was not the country for him to travel in, since you could only travel in it in funny little round carts, called *karjols*, which you must drive yourself, and that he was far too near-sighted for that. (I had instantly wondered at his double glasses, of a kind I had never seen before.)

Then somebody suggested that we should examine the works of art, which, in that solitude, we could delightfully do. Tennyson led us, and we stopped at any sculpture which attracted his notice. But the only remark which my memory has retained was made before the famous black bust of Antinous. Tennyson bent forward a little, and said, in his deep, slow voice, "Ah! this is the inscrutable Bithynian!" There was a pause, and then he added, gazing into the eyes of the bust: "If we knew what he knew, we should understand the ancient world." If I live to be a hundred years old, I shall still hear his rich tones as he said this, without emphasis, without affectation, as though he were speaking to himself. And soon after, the gates of heaven were closed, and I went down three flights of stairs to my hell of rotten morocco.

1911.

ALFRED TENNYSON

AFTER THE FUNERAL

As we filed slowly out of the Abbey on the afternoon of Wednesday, the 12th of October, 1892, there must have occurred to others, I think, as to myself, a whimsical and half-terrifying sense of the symbolic contrast between what we had left and what we emerged upon. Inside, the grey and vitreous atmosphere, the reverberations of music moaning somewhere out of sight, the bones and monuments of the noble dead, reverence, antiquity, beauty, rest. Outside, in the raw air, a tribe of hawkers urging upon the edges of a dense and inquisitive crowd a large sheet of pictures of the pursuit of a flea by a "lady," and more insidious salesmen doing a brisk trade in what they falsely pretended to be "Tennyson's last poem."

Next day we read in our newspapers affecting accounts of the emotion displayed by the vast crowds outside the Abbey – horny hands dashing away the tear, seamstresses holding the "the little green volumes" to their faces to hide their agitation. Happy for those who could see these things with their fairy telescopes out of the garrets of Fleet Street. I, alas! – though I sought assiduously – could mark nothing of the kind. Entering the Abbey, conducted by courteous policemen through unparalleled masses of the curious, we distinguished patience, good behaviour, cheerful and untiring inquisitiveness, a certain obvious gratitude for an incomprehensible spectacle provided by the authorities, but nothing else. And leaving the Abbey, as I say, the impression was one almost sinister in its abrupt transition. Poetry, authority, the grace and dignity of life, seemed to have been left behind us for ever in that twilight where Tennyson was sleeping with Chaucer and with Dryden.

In recording this impression I desire nothing so little as to appear censorious. Even the external part of the funeral at Westminster seemed, as was said of the similar scene which was enacted there nearly two hundred years ago, "a well-conducted and uncommon public ceremony, where the philosopher can find nothing to condemn, nor the satirist to ridicule." But the contrast between the outside and the inside of the Abbey, a contrast which may possibly have been merely whimsical in itself, served for a parable of the condition of poetry in England as the burial of Tennyson has left it. If it be only the outworn body of this glorious man which we have relinquished to the safeguard of the Minster, gathered to his peers in the fulness of time, we have no serious ground for apprehension, nor, after the first painful moment, even for sorrow. His harvest is ripe, and we hold it in our granaries. The noble physical presence which has been the revered companion of three generations has, indeed, sunk at length:

> Yet would we not disturb him from his tomb,
> Thus sleeping in his Abbey's friendly shade,
> And the rough waves of life for ever laid.

But what if this vast and sounding funeral should prove to have really been the entombment of English poetry? What if it should be the prestige of verse that we left behind us in the Abbey? That is a question which has issues far more serious than the death of any one man, no matter how majestic that man may be . . .

I have found myself depressed and terrified at an ebullition of popularity which seems to have struck almost everybody else with extreme satisfaction. It has been very natural that the stupendous honour apparently done to Tennyson, not merely by the few who always valued him, but by the many who might be supposed to stand outside his influence, has been welcomed with delight and enthusiasm. But what is so sinister a circumstance is the excessive character of this exhibition. I think of the funeral of Wordsworth at Grasmere, only forty-two years ago, with a score of persons gathering quietly under the low wall that fenced them from the brawling Rotha; and I turn to the spectacle of the 12th, the vast black crowd in the street, the ten thousand persons refused admission to the Abbey, the whole enormous popular manifestation. What does it mean? Is Tennyson, great as he is, a thousand times greater than Wordsworth? Has poetry, in forty years, risen at this ratio in the public estimation? The democracy, I fear, doth protest too much, and there is danger in this hollow reverence.

The danger takes this form. It may at any moment come to be held that the poet, were he the greatest that ever lived, was greater than [the] poetry; the artist more interesting than his art . . . Tennyson had grown to be by far the most mysterious, august, and singular figure in English society. He represented poetry, and the world now expects its poets to be as picturesque, as aged, and as individual as he was, or else it will pay poetry no attention. I fear, to be brief, that the personal, as distinguished from the purely literary, distinction of Tennyson may strike, for the time being, a serious blow at the vitality of poetry in this country.

Circumstances have combined, in a very curious way, to produce this result. If a supernatural power could be conceived as planning a scenic effect, it could hardly have arranged it in a manner more

54

telling, or more calculated to excite the popular imagination, than has been the case in the quick succession of the death of Matthew Arnold, of Robert Browning, and of Tennyson . . . A great poet was followed by a greater, and he by the greatest of the century, and all within five years . . .

The tone of criticism since the death of Tennyson has been very much what might, under the circumstances have been expected. Their efforts to overwhelm his coffin with lilies and roses have seemed paltry to the critics, unless they could succeed, at the same time, in laying waste all the smaller gardens of his neighbours. But when we come to think calmly on this matter, it will be seen that this offering up of the live poets as a burnt sacrifice to the memory of their dead master is absurd and grotesque. We have boasted all these years that we possessed the greatest of the world's poets since Victor Hugo. We did well to boast. But he is taken from us at a great age, and we complain at once, with bitter cries – because we have no poet left so venerable or so perfect in ripeness of the long-drawn years of craftsmanship – that poetry is dead amongst us, and that all the other excellent artists in verse are worthless scribblers. This is natural, perhaps, but it is scarcely generous and not a little ridiculous. It is, moreover, exactly what the critics said in 1850, when Arnold, Browning, and Tennyson had already published a great deal of their most admirable work.

The ingratitude of the hour towards the surviving poets of England pays but a poor compliment to the memory of that great man whose fame it professes to honour. I suppose that there has scarcely been a writer of interesting verse who has come into anything like prominence within the lifetime of Tennyson who has not received from him some letter of praise – some message of benevolent indulgence. More than fifty years ago he wrote, in glowing terms, to congratulate Mr Bailey on his *Festus*; it is only yesterday that we were hearing of his letters to Mr Rudyard Kipling and Mr William Watson. Tennyson did not affect to be a critic – no man, indeed, can ever have lived who less *affected* to be anything – but he loved good verses, and he knew them when he saw them, and welcomed them indulgently. No one can find it more distasteful to him to have it asserted that Tennyson was, and will be, "the last of the English poets" than would Tennyson himself.

It was not my good fortune to see him many times, and only twice, at an interval of about twelve years, did I have the privilege of hearing him talk at length and ease. On each of those occasions, however, it was noticeable with what warmth and confidence he spoke of the future of English poetry, with what interest he evidently followed its progress, and how cordially he appreciated what various younger men were doing. In particular, I hope it is not indiscreet to refer to the tone in which he spoke to me on each of these occasions of Mr Swinburne, whose critical conscience had, it must not be forgotten, led him to refer with no slight severity to several of the elder poet's writings. In 1877 Mr Swinburne's strictures were still recent, and might not unreasonably have been painfully recollected. Yet Tennyson spoke of him almost as Dryden did two hundred years ago to Congreve:

> And this I prophesy – thou shalt be seen
> (Though with some short parenthesis between)
> High on the throne of wit, and, seated there,
> Not mine (that's little), but thy laurel wear.

It would never have occurred to this great and wise man that his own death could be supposed to mark the final burning up and turning to ashes of the prophetic bays . . .

It was only in Paradise, so we learn from St Basil, that roses ever grew without thorns. We cannot have the rose of such an exceptional life as Tennyson's without suffering for it. We suffer by the void its cessation produces, the disturbance in our literary hierarchy that it brings, the sense of uncertainty and insufficiency that follows upon it. The death of Victor Hugo led to precisely such a rocking and swaying of the ship of literature in France, and to this day it cannot be said that the balance there is completely restored. I cannot think that we gain much by ignoring this disturbance, which is inevitable, and still less by folding our hands and calling out that it means that the vessel is sinking. It means nothing of the kind. What it does mean is that when a man of the very highest rank in the profession lives to an exceptionally great age, and retains his intellectual gifts to the end, combining with these unusual advantages the still more fortuitous ones of being singular and picturesque in his personality and the object of much ungratified curiosity, he becomes the victim, in the eyes of his contemporaries, of a sort of vertical mirage. He is seen up in the sky where no man could be. I trust I shall not be accused of anything like disrespect to the genius of Tennyson – which I loved and admired as nearly to the pitch of idolatry as possible – when I say that his reputation at this moment is largely mirage. His gifts were of the very highest order; but in the popular esteem, at this moment, he holds a position which is, to carry on the image, topographically impossible. No poet, no man, ever reached that altitude above his fellows.

The result of seeing one mountain in vertical mirage, and various surrounding acclivities (if that were possible) at their proper heights, would be to falsify the whole system of optical proportion. Yet this is what is now happening, and for some little time will continue to happen *in crescendo*, with regard to Tennyson and his surviving contemporaries. There is no need, however, to cherish "those gloomy thoughts led on by spleen" which the melancholy events of the past month have awakened. The recuperative force of the arts has never yet failed the human race, and will not fail us now. All the *Tit-Bits* and *Pearson's Weeklies* in the world will not be able to destroy a fragment of pure and original literature, although the tastes they foster may delay its recognition and curtail its rewards.

The duty of all who have any influence on the public is now clear. So far from resigning the responsibility of praise and blame, so far from opening the flood-gates to what is bad – on the ground that the best is gone, and that it does not matter – it behoves those who are our recognized judges of literary merit to resist more strenuously than ever the inroads of mere commercial success into the Temple of Fame. The Scotch ministry preserve that interesting practice of "fencing the tables" of the Lord by a solemn searching of would-be communicants. Let the tables of Apollo be fenced, not to the exclusion or the discomfort of those who have a right to his sacraments, but to the chastening of those who have no other mark of his service but their passbook. And poetry, which survived the death of Chaucer, will recover even from the death of Tennyson.

1892.

TWENTY-SIX YEARS ON

[In] the appendix of "Impressions", by a series of elderly friends, which closes the official *Life of Tennyson*, published in 1897, [the reader] will find there an expression of the purest Victorian optimism. The great object being to foist on the public a false and superhuman picture of the deceased, a set of illustrious contemporaries – who themselves expected to be, when they died, transfigured in like manner – form a bodyguard around the corpse of the poet and emit their "tedious panegyric". In this case, more even than in any of the instances which Mr Strachey has taken, the contrast between the real man and the funereal image is positively grotesque.

Without question this contrast is not a little responsible for the discredit into which the name of Tennyson has fallen. Lord Selbourne found nothing in Tennyson "inconsistent with the finest courtesy and the gentlest heart." Dr Jowett had preserved through forty years "an ever-increasing wonder at the depth of his thought", and emphatically stated that he "was above such feelings as a desire of praise, or fear of blame." (Tennyson, who was thirsty for ceaseless laudation, and to whom a hint of censure was like the bite of a mosquito!). Frederick Myers ejaculated, "How august, how limitless a thing was Tennyson's own spirit's upward flight!" The Duke of Argyll, again, during the space of forty years, had found him "always reverent, hating all levity or flippancy," and was struck by his possessing "the noblest humility I have ever known." Lord Macaulay, who "had stood absolutely aloof", once having been permitted to glance at the proof-sheets of *Guenevere*, was "absolutely subdued" to "unfeigned and reverent admiration". The duke was the glad emissary who was "the medium of introduction," and he recognized in Macaulay's subjugation "a premonition" of Tennyson's complete "conquest over the living world and over the generations that are to come."

Thus the priesthood circled round their idol, waving their censers and shouting their hymns of praise, while their ample draperies effectively hid from the public eye the object which was really in the centre of their throng, namely, a gaunt, black, touzled man, rough in speech, brooding like an old gypsy over his inch of clay pipe stuffed with shag, and sucking in port wine with gusto – "so long as it is black and sweet and strong, I care not!" Their fault lay, not in their praise, which was much of it deserved, but in their deliberate attempt in the interests of what was Nice and Proper – gods of the Victorian Age – to conceal what any conventional person might think not quite becoming. There were to be no shadows in the picture, no stains or rugosities on the smooth bust of rosy wax.

1918.

Algernon Swinburne

1837–1909

The young Edmund Gosse had been reading Swinburne for years, and had seen him on more than one occasion, when they first met at the house of Ford Madox Brown in December 1870. Gosse was then just 21 and had recently published his first book. It was Swinburne, it seems, who ultimately released the younger man from the powerful hold of his father and the overwhelming religion in which he had been brought up. There is no question that Gosse loved Swinburne, the man he called "our greatest living poet", the man who, as Hardy pointed out, had damned himself in many people's eyes with one memorable phrase: "the supreme evil, God". In the seventies Gosse described himself as his "faithful henchman", but there would come a time, going through Swinburne's papers after the poet's death in 1909, when he had to admit: "I confess that Swinburne occasionally makes me physically sick."

Gosse's first biographical account of Swinburne was for the 1912 *Dictionary of National Biography*. This piece was privately printed at the Chiswick Press in an edition of 50 copies and subsequently appeared in *Portraits and Sketches*, later the same year. The first pages here are part of that version. Gosse had his own copy of the Chiswick Press pamphlet interleaved "with a view to constant correction and addition". It was "a sort of stock on which to graft exact biographical information". But the trouble was that, as he found out more and more about his old hero, Gosse realized much of it was unpublishable. He told T J Wise they should "try to prevent the world from ever learning what a pig he sometimes was".

When Gosse eventually published his carefully self-censored *Life of Swinburne*, his last major book, he was criticized by a number of people whose opinion he respected, as he explains in the *Confidential Paper*. He then decided to lodge this in the British Museum, putting down his own knowledge of the more scandalous aspects of Swinburne's life, notably his alcoholism and his taste for flagellation. Even here he does not face up to or explore the question of Swinburne's sexual orientation. The paper was first published by C Y Lang in his Yale edition of Swinburne's letters and is reproduced here by permission of Edmund Gosse's granddaughter and literary executor, Jennifer Gosse.

*   *   *

The extraordinary reputation of Swinburne in the later sixties was constructed of several elements. It was built up on the legend of his mysterious and unprecedented physical appearance, of the astonishing verbal beauty of his writings, but most of all on his defiance of the intellectual and religious prejudices of his age and generation. He was not merely a poet, but a flag; and not merely a flag, but the Red Flag incarnate. There was an idea abroad, and it was not ill-founded, that in matters of taste the age in England had for some time been stationary, if not stagnant. It was necessary to wake people up; as Victor Hugo had said: "Il faut rudoyer le genre humain," and in every gesture it was believed that Swinburne set forth to "rudoyer" the Philistines. This was welcome to all young persons sitting in bondage, who looked up to Swinburne as to the deliverer . . .

My earliest letter from Swinburne was dated September 14, 1867, when I was still in my eighteenth year, and I first saw him in 1868 . . . It was in the evening of July 10, 1868, that I first cast eyes on the poet who was at that time the divinity, the object of feverish worship, to every budding artist and faltering singer in England. The occasion was accidental, the circumstances painful; it is enough to say that the idol was revealed to the juvenile worshipper at a startling moment of physical suffering and distress, and that the impression was one of curious terror, never, even under happier auspices, to be wholly removed. I shall not lose that earliest, and entirely unanticipated, image of a languishing and pain-stricken Swinburne, like some odd conception of Aubrey Beardsley, a *Cupido crucifixus* on a chair of anguish . . .

I was not presented to him, however, until the last week in 1870, when, in a note from the kind hostess who brought us together, I find it stated: "Algernon took to you at once, as is seldom the case with him." In spite of this happy beginning, the acquaintance remained superficial until 1873, when, I hardly know how, it ripened suddenly into an intimate friendship. From that time until he left London for good in the autumn of 1879 I saw

Swinburne very frequently indeed, and for several years later than that our intercourse continued to be close. These relations were never interrupted, except by his increasing deafness and general disinclination to leave home. I would, then, say that the memories I venture to bring forward deal mainly with the years from 1873 to 1880, but extend a little before and after that date . . .

In the days when I watched him closely I found myself constantly startled by the physical problem: What place has this singular being in the *genus homo*? It would easily be settled by the vague formula of "degeneration," but to a careful eye there was nothing in Swinburne of what is known as the debased or perverse type. The stigmata of the degenerate, such as we have been taught to note them, were entirely absent. Here were, to the outward and untechnical perception at least, no radical effects of disease, hereditary or acquired. He stood on a different physical footing from other men; he formed, as Cowley said of Pindar, "a vast species alone." If there had been a planet peopled by Swinburnes, he would have passed as an active, healthy, normal specimen of it. All that was extraordinary in him was not, apparently, the result of ill-health, but of individual and inborn peculiarity.

The world is familiar from portraits, and still better from caricatures, with his unique appearance. He was short, with sloping shoulders, from which rose a long and slender neck, surmounted by a very large head. The cranium seemed to be out of all proportion to the rest of the structure. His spine was rigid, and though he often bowed the heaviness of his head, *lasso papavera collo*, he seemed never to bend his back. Except in consequence of a certain physical weakness, which probably may, in more philosophical days, come to be accounted for and palliated – except when suffering from this external cause, he seemed immune from all the maladies that pursue mankind. He did not know fatigue; his agility and brightness were almost mechanical. I never heard him complain of a headache or of a toothache. He required very little sleep, and occasionally when I have parted from him in the evening after saying "Good-night," he has simply sat back in the deep sofa in his sitting-room, his little feet close together, his arms against his side, folded in his frock-coat like a grasshopper in its wing-covers, and fallen asleep, apparently for the night, before I could blow out the candles and steal forth from the door. I am speaking, of course, of early days; it was thus about 1875 that I closely observed him.

He was more a hypertrophied intelligence than a man. His vast brain seemed to weigh down and give solidity to a frame otherwise as light as thistledown, a body almost as immaterial as that of a fairy. In the streets he had the movements of a somnambulist, and often I have seen him passing like a ghost across the traffic of Holborn, or threading the pressure of carts eastward in Gray's Inn Road, without glancing to the left or the right, like something blown before a wind. At that time I held a humble post at the British Museum, from which I was freed at four o'clock, and Swinburne liked to arrange to meet me half-way between that monument and his own lodgings. One of Swinburne's peculiarities was an extreme punctuality, and we seldom failed to meet on the deserted northern pavement of Great Coram Street. But although the meeting was of his own making, and the person to be met a friend seen every day, if I stood a couple of yards before him silent, he would endeavour to escape on one side and then on the other, giving a great shout of satisfaction when at length his eyes focused on my face . . .

No physiologist who studied the corporeal condition of Swinburne could avoid observing the violent elevation of spirits to which he was constantly subject. The slightest emotional excitement, of anger, or pleasure, or admiration, sent him into a state which could scarcely be called anything but convulsive. He was like that little geyser in Iceland which is always simmering, but which if it is irritated by having pieces of turf thrown into it, instantly boils over and flings its menacing column at the sky. I was never able to persuade myself whether the extraordinary spasmodic action of the arms and legs which accompanied these paroxysms was the result of nature or habit. It was violent and it was long-continued, but I never saw that it produced fatigue. It gradually subsided into a graceful and smiling calm, sometimes even into somnolence, out of which, however, a provocative remark would instantly call up again the surprising spasm of the geyser . . . Swinburne seemed to me to divide his hours between violent cerebral excitement and sheer immobility, mental and physical. He would sit for a long time together without stirring a limb, his eyes fixed in a sort of trance, and only his lips shifting and shivering a little, without a sound.

The conception of Swinburne, indeed, as incessantly flamboyant and convulsive is so common that it may be of value to note that he was, on the contrary, sometimes pathetically plaintive and distressed. The following impression, written down next day (January 4, 1878), reveals a Swinburne little imagined by the public, but frequently enough to be observed in those days by intimate friends. It describes a slightly later condition than that on which I have hitherto dwelt:

"Swinburne has become very much at home with us, and, knowing our eating-times, he drops in every fortnight or so to dinner, and stays through the evening. All this winter he has been noticeably worn and feeble, sometimes tottering like an old man, and glad to accept a hand to help him up and down stairs. I hear he is very violent between whiles, but he generally visits us during the exhaustion and depression which follow his fits of excitement, when he is tired of his loneliness at Great James Street, and seems to crave the comfort of home-life and the petting that we lavish on him. Last night he arrived about 5 P.M.; he was waiting for me when I came back from the office. The maid had seen him into my study, brightened the fire and raised the lamp, but although she left him cosily seated under the light, I found him mournfully wandering, like a lost thing, on the staircase. We happened to be quite alone, and he stayed on for six hours. He was extremely gentle, bright, and sensible at dinner, full of gay talk about early memories, his recollections of Dickens, and odd anecdotes of older Oxford friends. Directly dinner was over he insisted on seeing the baby, whom on these occasions he always kisses, and worships on his knees, and is very fantastic over. When he and I were alone, he closed up to the fire, his great head bowed, his knees held tight together, and his finger-tips pressed to his chest, in what I call his 'penitential' attitude, and he began a long tale, plaintive and rather vague, about his loneliness, the sadness of his life, the suffering he experiences from the slanders of others. He said that George Eliot was hounding on her myrmidons to his destruction. I made out that this referred to some attack in a newspaper which he supposes, very groundlessly I expect, to be inspired by George Eliot. Swinburne said that a little while ago he found his intellectual energy succumbing under a morbid distress at his isolation, and that he had been obliged steadily to review before his conscience his imaginative life in order to prevent himself from sinking into despair. This is only a mood, to be sure; but if there be any people who think so ill of him, I only wish they could see him as we see him at these recuperative intervals. Whatever he may be elsewhere, in our household not a kinder, simpler, or more affectionate creature could be desired as a visitor. The only fault we find with him is that his little mournful ways and his fragility drag painfully upon our sympathy."

This, it will be admitted, is not the Swinburne of legend in the seventies, and that it is so different may be judged, I hope, my excuse for recording it. A very sensible further change came over him when he was attacked by deafness, an infirmity to which, I believe, most members of his family have been liable. I do not think that I noticed any hardness of hearing until 1880, when the affliction rapidly developed. He was, naturally, very much concerned at it, and in the summer of that year he wrote to a lady of my household, "If this gets worse I shall become wholly unfit to mix in any society where two or three are gathered together." It did get worse; it was constitutional and incurable, and for the last quarter of a century of his life he was almost impervious to outward sound. All the more, therefore, was he dependent on the care of the devoted friend who thenceforward guarded him so tenderly.

*

The conversation of Swinburne, in the days of his youth and power, was very splendid in quality. No part of a great man disappears so completely as his table-talk, and of nothing is it more difficult afterwards to reconstruct an impression. Swinburne's conversation had, as was to be expected, some of the characteristics of his poetry. It was rapid, and yet not voluble; it was measured, ornate, and picturesque, and yet it was in a sense homely. It was much less stilted and involved than his prose writing. His extreme natural politeness was always apparent in his talk, unless, of course, some unfortunate *contretemps* should rouse a sudden ebullition, when he could be neither just nor kind. But, as a rule, his courtesy shone out of his blue-grey eyes and was lighted up by the halo of his cloud of orange hair as he waved it, gravely or waggishly, at the company . . .

His feeling about literature was serious to the verge of fanaticism. It absorbed him like a religion, and it was this unflagging sense of the superhuman power and value of poetry which made his conversation so stimulating, especially to a very young man whom he honoured with the untrammelled expression of his opinions. But he had a charming delicacy of toleration for the feelings of those whom he respected, even when he believed them to be tainted with error.

Outside poetry, and, in lesser measure, his family life, Swinburne's interests were curiously limited. He had no "small talk," and during the discussion of the common topics of the day his attention at once flagged and fell off, the glazed eyes betraying that the mind was far away. For science he had no taste whatever,

64

and his lack of musical ear was a byword among his acquaintances. I once witnessed a practical joke played upon him, which made me indignant at the time, but which now seems innocent enough, and not without interest. A lady, having taken the rest of the company into her confidence, told Swinburne that she would render on the piano a very ancient Florentine ritornello which had just been discovered. She then played "Three Blind Mice," and Swinburne was enchanted. He found that it reflected to perfection the cruel beauty of the Medicis – which perhaps it does. But this exemplifies the fact that all impressions with him were intellectual, and that an appeal to his imagination would gild the most common object with romance.

In the days I speak of, Swinburne lived in large, rather empty rooms on the first floor of an old house in Great James Street, which used to remind me of one of Dickens's London houses in "Great Expectations" or "Little Dorrit." But until the death of his father, who died at a great age in the early autumn of 1877, Swinburne always had a country home in Holmwood, near Henley-on-Thames. At Admiral Swinburne's death I think he stayed on with his mother at Holmwood till the end of that year. Such months on the banks of the Thames were always beneficial to his health, and he wrote there without interruption. I find a note (1875): "How exuberant S. always is when he comes back; it is partly pleasure at being in London again, and partly refreshment from his country captivity." Of his visits to the sea-coast of Norfolk and Suffolk others must speak, for I never had the pleasure of accompanying him.

When he came back from the country to town he was always particularly anxious to recite or read aloud his own poems. In doing this he often became very much excited, and even, in his overwhelming sense of the movement of the metre, would jump about the room in a manner somewhat embarrassing to the listener. His method of procedure was uniform. He would arrive at a friend's house with a breast-pocket obviously bulging with manuscript but buttoned across his chest. After floating about the room and greeting his host and hostess with many little becks of the head, and affectionate smiles, and light wavings of the fingers, he would settle at last upright on a chair, or, by preference, on a sofa, and sit there in a state of rigid immobility, the toe of one foot pressed against the heel of the other. Then he would say, in an airy, detached way, as though speaking of some absent person, "I have brought with me my 'Thalassius' or my 'Wasted Garden' (or whatever it might happen to be), which I have just finished."

Then he would be folded again in silence, looking at nothing. We then were to say, "Oh, do please read it to us! Will you?" Swinburne would promptly reply, "I had no intention in the world of boring you with it, but since you ask me –" and out would come the MS. I do not remember that there was ever any variation in this little ceremony, which sometimes preluded many hours of recitation and reading. His delivery, especially of his own poetry, was delightful as long as he sat quietly in his seat. His voice, which was of extraordinary beauty, "the pure Ashburnham voice," as his cousin explains to me, rose and fell monotonously, but with a flute-like note which was very agreeable, and the pulse of the rhythm was strongly yet delicately felt. I shall never forget the successive evenings on which he read "Bothwell" aloud in his lodgings, in particular one on which Edward Burne-Jones, Arthur O'Shaughnessy, P B Marston, and I sat with him at his round marble-topped table – lighted only by candles in two giant candlesticks of serpentine he had brought from the Lizard – and heard him read the magnificent second act of that tragedy. He surpassed himself in vigour and melody of utterance that night. But sometimes, in reading, he lost control of his emotions, the sound became a scream, and he would dance about the room, the paper fluttering from his finger-tips like a pennon in a gale of wind . . .

The sound of Swinburne wailing forth in his thrilling semitones such stanzas as that addressed to the Sea:

> I shall sleep, and move with the moving ships,
>   Change as the winds change, veer in the tide;
> My lips will feast on the foam of thy lips,
>   I shall rise with thy rising, with thee subside;
> Sleep, and not know if she be, if she were,
> Filled full with life to the eyes and hair,
> As a rose is fulfilled to the roseleaf tips
>   With splendid summer and perfume and pride,

is something which will not fade out of memory as long as life lasts.

1909–12.

THE CONFIDENTIAL PAPER

After the publication of my "Life of Swinburne," the fact that I had passed vaguely, and in terms which left all detail to be conjectured, over the moral irregularities of the poet, was animadverted upon severely by some of the reviewers, and caused, I was told, an undefined sense of "disappointment." So far as this was merely the result of foiled curiosity, I was unmoved, but the censure of certain friends, expressed in private, and with great courtesy, has induced me to feel that I have a duty to posterity, and that I ought not, as the chief and almost the only surviving depositary of exact knowledge about Swinburne, to leave the matter unfixed and liable to error in the minds of serious persons. I have therefore decided to write down, with closest attention to the truth as I recall it, or have been able to collect it, the physical characteristics of this extraordinary man. I trust that all who read these words will consider that they are presented to them in confidence, and will use them only to guard the memory of the poet from unnecessary obloquy. If they find anything here to distress them, let them on the other hand be persuaded that they now know the worst. If legend should present the facts in another, or in a more disagreeable light, let them be sure that so far as I have been able, in the strictest scrutiny, to discover, what legend says and what I do not confirm is not true.

First, I would explain why a particular reticence was forced upon me. I will not dwell unduly on the fact that Swinburne was a generous friend and a very fine gentleman, and that it seemed to devolve upon me not to betray his secrets to the coarse public, nor to render him an object of ridicule and disgust. The conditions which I will now describe were of a nature, if put crudely before a commonplace audience, to seem much more flagitious and much more degrading than they really were. Let me be emphatic on one point. Extravagant, even vicious, as might be some sides of Swinburne's conduct, they were not essential, but accidental; that is to say, they might have been entirely absent without the nature of his genius being affected by that absence. I do not say that they did not influence some portion of his early work, but they might have done so exactly as much as if they had been, so far as the world could judge, entirely interior and not visible to the closest observer. They were no part of his genius, and scarcely an excrescence upon it. The two painful and disgraceful forms of indulgence which I am about to describe had no more to do with the inner character of Swinburne than the laudanum had to do with the inner character of De Quincey. It is even possible to suppose that they responded to some strange requirement of his very unusual physical conformation. In conversation, he never boasted of them, or even acknowledged their existence. They existed, as it were, outside his morality, which was in all essentials (strange as it may sound) unaffected by them. He was totally without the vicious desire to cause other persons to accept his conduct in these matters as admirable. He never excused, or boasted, or expressed any remorse or regret for these excesses. I never heard him, and I never heard of anyone else who heard him, recommend them to others. He was a perfectly safe companion for youth, and to those who were temperate and innocent he seemed to have himself preserved both temperance and innocence. This very strange fact was much in my mind when I refrained from giving my narrative the sensational colouring with which I might so easily have heightened its interest. I could not have told part of the truth without involving myself in subtleties which would have been more bewildering to ordinary readers than reticence itself.

*

When Swinburne died in 1909, the only survivor of his immediate family was his youngest sister, Miss Isabel Swinburne. But she was in the closest relation with her – and his – first cousin, Mrs Disney Leith, who came forward immediately with a series of valuable, and abundant, but somewhat inexact "recollections" of his childhood. Since his early manhood Mrs Disney Leith had scarcely seen him, but she now constituted herself the protector of his memory . . . There was a sort of conspiracy that Algernon should be presented to posterity as a guileless and featureless model of respectability . . .

Lord Redesdale, although in his 80th year, went down to the Isle of Wight on purpose to see his cousin, Mrs Disney Leith, and to persuade her to receive me. She positively refused to do so, and the utmost which Lord Redesdale could induce her to concede was to read the first chapter of my "Life" in MS, and this only if it was brought her by Lord Redesdale and returned by her to him, so that she should come into no contact with me. This was carried out. Mrs Disney Leith was quite open in her line of action. She objected to: 1) the assumption that Algernon was irreligious ("he was in communion with the Church of England all his life," she declared); 2) the suggestion that he drank ("he was never intoxicated in all his life," she said); and 3) she, and Miss Isabel in her wake passively, were infuriated at what I had said about Swinburne's relation with Adah Isaacs Menken. Mrs Leith had the naïveté to say, to the very great amusement of Lord Redesdale,

"Algernon was far too well-bred a gentleman ever to *speak* to a woman of that class!"

The family, thus actuated by an intense determination to reduce the poet to a respectable commonplace, offered me a resistance which was quite formidable. Not merely did they refuse to help me in any degree, but they sent me the message that if I published anything "unpleasant" they should denounce the whole of my narrative as "a pack of falsehoods," without going into particulars. This would put a biographer, who must be helpless in a fight with a group of aged but determined ladies, in a deplorable position, and both Mr Wise and Lord Redesdale, – and later Lord Crewe to whom in this predicament I applied for practical counsel, – advised me to refrain as much as I possibly could from statements which might infuriate the enemy . . .

During the central years of his life Swinburne was a drunkard. I have not been able, in spite of the closest examination of survivors, to discover when he first gave way to wine. A story of his having been drunk at Eton faded under pressure into nothing more than a report of his odd ways and excited gestures. Those who were with him at Oxford – such as Lord Bryce, who knew him intimately, and Lord Sheffield, – are unable to recollect that he was ever the worse for liquor there, or was more excited than other lads at such few college "wines" as he took part in. I have not found any distinct evidence of his being scandalously drunk until about 1862, and even this is questionable. Lord Redesdale believed it was Richard Burton – who introduced him to brandy, which he had scarcely tasted before, – whose influence did A.C.S. most harm in this direction. At all events, by 1864 or 65, the habit had completely seized Swinburne, and gave all his best friends distress and alarm. It continued until he was taken down to Putney in 1879, then completely overmastered by it, and rendered unfit for decent society.

Lord Houghton, after Burton had gone off to Brazil, ventured, in August 1865, to expostulate with Swinburne on the increasing danger he ran from abuse of alcohol, and to suggest to him that now "the tempter" had set sail, he should turn over a new page. In replying, Swinburne admitted that "it is not given to all his juniors to *tenir tête à* Burton," but continued "I deny that his hospitality ever succeeded in upsetting me – as he himself on the morrow of a latish séance admitted with approbation, allowing that he had thought to get me off my legs." This is a good instance of Swinburne's marvellous gift for self-deception. Nothing was so easy as to "get him off his legs," but he never appeared to be

69

aware of it himself. Indeed, I doubt whether, to the very end, he distinctly identified his state of health with his alcoholic indulgences. In his letters, he occasionally speaks of other victims of inebriety with sorrow and pain, not priggishly, but as one who sincerely grieves that a friend should allow himself to be overcome with wine. These expressions seem to be those of a man, who is all mercy to the weakness of others, but has no temptation of the same kind himself, and who deplores what he takes credit to himself for not sharing. There was not an iota of hypocrisy in this. Swinburne, as I have carefully noted on many occasions, really did not know that he was a drunkard.

This needs explanation, and may seem incredible. But he succumbed so rapidly and so suddenly to a slight excess of alcohol that he was like a person who has taken laughing gas. When such a man comes back to consciousness he recollects nothing. Swinburne would be sober one moment, and quite drunk the next – quite drunk, yet able still to talk, recite, and alas! to shout. But I have often observed that his recollection ceased at a moment before the sudden inebriation, and his memory would be of having been very happy and gay, perhaps a little too gay, and then of waking up with a headache or an indigestion which he attributed to the lobster or the cucumber.

As an example of this power of persistent self-deception, I may give a single anecdote. He was dining alone with my Wife and myself at a time (September 10, 1877) when his habits were a matter of scandal to the public and embarrassment to his friends. I perceived at dinner that Algernon was reaching the danger-point. I had taken the precaution of putting the decanter away, and when, after several disregarded hints, the poet asked for more wine, I grossly lied and said there was no more in the house, going out of the room in a pretended search. This was clumsily done, and even Swinburne saw through the pretence of it. When I came back to announce my inability to find another drop, my Wife was half weeping with mingled emotions of hospitality and duty, for Swinburne had sidled along the table towards her, and had said, slowly and in a low voice, while gazing into her eyes with an air of reproachful innocence, "Does Edmund really think it *possible* that I could ever be so little of a gentleman as to drink more than was good for me?" We were, however, firm, and my Wife, for whom Swinburne had a great affection and a great respect, managed to divert his thoughts, so that the craving passed away, and he spent with us an evening of charming conversation. This should carefully be noted – that Swinburne was much affected by the pressure of other minds. When he was at Holmwood, for months at a time, under the protection of his mother and father, I believe that he very rarely "exceeded"; but in the company of a toper, he "toped" at once. Lord Redesdale told me that at some studio-party – I think at Whistler's, before the painter went off to Valparaiso, – all the men were smoking, but no drink was provided. Swinburne stood silent and rigid, till suddenly he screamed out, "Moi, je ne fume jamais, mais je BOIS." Nobody responded, however, or brought him any alcohol, and he presently forgot it. The influence of Watts-Dunton, who kept him temperate for thirty years without any complete prohibition, is a case in point . . .

It was important, at meals, to keep the wine or beer or spirits out of Swinburne's reach. If this were not done, as often by host or hostesses not aware of his weakness, he would gradually fix his stare upon the bottle as if he wished to fascinate it, and then, in a moment, flash or pounce upon it, like a mongoose on a snake, drawing it towards him as though it resisted and had to be struggled with. Then, if no one had the presence of mind to interfere, a tumbler was filled in a moment, and Swinburne had drained it to the last drop, sucking-in the liquid with a sort of fiery gluttony, tilting the glass into his shaking lips, and violently opening and shutting his eyelids. It was an extraordinary sight, and one which never failed to fill me with alarm, for after that the Bacchic transition might come at any moment.

In 1869, I think, – Swinburne formed a very undesirable acquaintance with Charles Duncan Cameron, a man some ten or a dozen years older than himself. Cameron, after a stormy life in several parts of Africa, had settled in Abyssinia, where he became some sort of Consul, and attracted the enmity of the notorious King Theodore, who imprisoned him for about four years. He was released at last, and arriving in London during the summer of 1868 became a nine-days' wonder, and was much fêted on account of his adventures. I never saw him, but I heard a good deal in disfavour of his moral character – although he was said to be a very diverting companion. How Swinburne came to know him, I have never heard, but they were on terms of considerable familiarity. Among other things, Cameron "drank like a fish," and on one occasion in the spring of 1870, he was Swinburne's guest to dinner at the Arts' Club. They planned to go to some entertainment together, and so dined early. They got extremely drunk, and when they left the table, and went to the garde-robe, the room was hung with the hats of other diners, – no doubt, tall silk hats which everybody wore then. Swinburne could not find his hat, which, on account of the great size of his head, was of excessive capacity. He tried one hat after another, and as each pinched his brows he flung it to the floor; finally, in a towering and ungovernable rage, he danced and stamped upon the hats. There had been a good deal of complaint of his behaviour in the Club already, and this was too much; he was asked to resign, as I have mentioned, without giving the details, on page 198 of the "Life." Cameron presently disappeared from England, under a cloud as I believe, and died very shortly after in Switzerland.

Speaking of hats reminds me of a droll spectacle I enjoyed in 1872, I think, or perhaps a little earlier. I was talking with W Bell Scott in the embrasure of the bow-window on the first floor of his house in Cheyne Walk, when a hansom-cab drew up at the front door below us. Nothing happened at first, and then Walter Pater, delicately dressed, with lemon-yellow kid gloves, descended daintily, and was followed by Swinburne, who poised himself on the edge of the cab, and then dived forward on to the pavement, descending upon his two hands. His elegant top-hat sprang from him, and making a wide curve descended far away in the gutter. Presently Pater appeared in our upper room, talking with dreamy detachment on indifferent subjects, but of Swinburne I saw no more, and understood that he was taken into another part of the house to be cleaned and sobered.

For a long time, his bouts of abandonment to drink were occasional and brief, but they gradually grew more lengthy as well as more frequent. At the time when he was forcibly removed from his lodgings by Theodore Watts, his condition had become deplorable and disgusting beyond words. He had developed the symptoms of delirium tremens, and that he should recover at all, more still that he should recover so completely, astonished the doctors. He did recover; nevertheless, it is certain that there was something luminous and vivid which was quenched in his nature, and that never reappeared after 1879.

*

I believe that the generative instinct was very feebly developed in Swinburne. When I walked about London with him by day and night, I was struck with the fact that he never seemed to observe the faces or figures of people whom we met, or to receive from them any of those electric shocks which are the torment and ecstasy of youth. He was fond of the society of women, but without what could be called fatuity, and he was never known so far as I have seen or heard, to indulge in the least flirtation. He occasionally remarked on the form of a woman, or her colouring, but always as he would speak of a work of art, and generally with a reference to some painter. I remember his saying to my Wife, whose colour of complexion and hair was brilliant "I used to think you should have been painted by Titian, but now I see that it should have been Paris Bordone!" His manner with women was very courteous, rather formal, with a sort of intellectual assiduity, never in any degree suggesting the amorous, or as though love entered his mind. I have seen advances made to him, but he neither accepted nor repulsed them; he simply seemed not to perceive them. He was rather like a child, who witnesses the embracements of grown-up people without interest and without perturbation.

In the days of his great celebrity, there were several women who would have been glad to attract his attention. In particular, the Jewish poetess Mathilde Blind, from about 1867 onwards, openly "threw herself at his head," and gave him every opportunity to propose marriage to her. She complained, in my presence, of his insensibility; "he comes to tea with me, and does not seem to notice, and he recites poetry, and goes away!" she said. He cultivated her company for the sake of her regicide principles and her love of verse; her brother was the Ferdinand Cohen who tried to kill Bismarck, and her step-father was the revolutionary Karl Blind. Mathilde used to say that she was the possessor of "lots of wonderful letters" from Swinburne, but, long afterwards, when the infatuation had passed away, and she sold these letters, it was found that they contained no word of love.

It is quite impossible for me to form a conjecture how far generative instinct entered into the very disagreeable and unintelligible peculiarity which I am now obliged to mention. If no proofs of this strange weakness were in existence, it would be desirable to ignore it, and to destroy in silence any evidence which might possibly tend to its discovery. But Swinburne's letters, and even some of his published works, teem with indications of it, to such a degree that it will be very difficult to prevent some rash editor of the future, some youthful enthusiast ignorant of the odd turns which life takes, from blurting out the truth without knowing what he is talking about. I find the greatest difficulty in describing what the matter with Swinburne was, because, as is obvious, the whole thing is obscure and unaccountable. What is curious is that a doubt must ever remain whether the excitement he received was wholly or only partly sexual. Let it be said, then, that he not only liked to be whipped, but he experienced an ecstatic pleasure in letting his mind rest on flagellation, and in conjuring up scenes of it. He said that the taste for this punishment had come to him at Eton, and he wrote, in 1863, "Once, before giving me a swishing that I had the marks of for more than a month, [the tutor] let me saturate my face with eau-de-cologne . . . He meant to stimulate and excite the senses by that preliminary pleasure so as to inflict the acuter pain afterwards on their awakened and intensified susceptibility . . . He was a stunning tutor; his one other pet subject was *metre*, and I fairly believe that my ear for verses made me rather a favourite. I can boast that of all the swishings I ever had up to seventeen and over, I never had one for a false quantity; I made it up in arithmetic."

This mania for suffering pain, whatever it was, I think remained dormant until 1861, when it was violently developed by Swinburne's borrowing and gloating over that atrocious book by the Marquis de Sade, "Justine; ou les Malheurs de la Vertu." For some time, for months and even years, allusions and quotations from this book, in Swinburne's correspondence, show what a profound impression it made on his mind, and I would warn those who come after me to exercise the greatest discretion in dealing with the various pseudonyms and false signatures which are strewn over his private letters and really deal with this subject. I do not think I am wrong in giving so much importance to the reading of *Justine*, since Swinburne's own horrible poem in French, called "Charenton," came into existence immediately after he borrowed that particular book; De Sade certainly quickened the habit of gloating over pain, and the desire of submitting to it. D G Rossetti, from whom Swinburne had no secrets, was fully aware of his appetite for flagellation, and of the excitement which the mere idea of it caused him.

"Charenton en 1810" was a poem in 112 lines, written in French alexandrines, and dated "Dimanche, 27 Octobre 1861." It described a vision in which the Marquis de Sade appeared to the author, "un jeune homme âgé de vingt-quatre ans"; – "cet enfant lisait ce jour *Justine*," and

> Il levait ses regards, comme on fait en priant,
> De la page proscrite au vieillard souriant.

Some years later than this, when he was living near Dorset Square, Swinburne was intimate with Savile Clark. One evening, when the poet was visiting S C, the latter went down to the kitchen of the lodging-house and found there a boy who was reciting Milton's *Paradise Lost*, and he fetched Swinburne to listen to him. The boy was John Thomson, of whom George R Sims has given an account in his *Reminiscences*. He was a great enthusiast for poetry, although only half-educated, and he considered it the greatest event of his life to be introduced to the author of *Poems and Ballads*. He contrived to secure a certain intimacy with the poet, who introduced him to the other pre-raphaelites, in particular to D G Rossetti, who took some notice of him. John Thomson had an interest (Sims tells me that it was perhaps a share) in a mysterious house in St John's Wood where two golden-haired and rouge-cheeked ladies received, in luxuriously furnished rooms, gentlemen whom they consented to chastise for large sums. Thomson introduced Swinburne to this establishment and he became a regular visitor. There was an elder lady, very respectable, who welcomed the guests and took the money. Swinburne much impoverished himself in these games, which also must have been very bad for his health.

The establishment in St John's Wood was shut up for a time, while the ladies went to Paris. In order to break him completely of his degrading and ignominious habit, D G Rossetti consulted one or two very intimate friends, who advised that he should be taken in hand by some sensible young woman who would "make a man of him," since he was known to have never had any physical connection, which, as Rossetti said, was ridiculous in the author of so many "voluptuous" poems. It should have been done sooner, for he was already nearly thirty-one years of age.

*

It was in the summer, I think, of 1867, that London went mad over the performance of a Miss Adah Isaacs Menken, who was carried round the stage in tights bound to the back of a very tame horse, as "Mazeppa." Her face was no longer particularly handsome, but she had a very fine figure. She was not much more than thirty, but she had been married many times, and now was dispensing with a husband. She was a strange admixture of coarseness and good-natured sensibility; she had lived with prize-fighters, and she wrote reams of lachrymose yearning poetry. It was agreed at Chelsea that she would be approached, and that she should be induced to take up the case of Algernon. In this curious affair, John Thomson was the go-between at Rossetti's instigation. Swinburne was taken to see her act in "Mazeppa," and her beauties were pointed out to him; it was further explained that she was a poetess and that she had a tremendous admiration for him. When his vanity was completely awakened, she paid him a visit, and according to his own account, then and there spent the night with him. She either lived altogether, or was a very frequent visitor, at his lodgings for some time, and they were very friendly indeed, but as Miss Menken apologetically observed to D G R, she didn't know how it was, but she hadn't been able to get him "up to the scratch," and so felt she must leave him.

The episode lasted for about six weeks, from the middle of December 1867 to February 1868. On the 26th of January Swinburne wrote "I must send you in a day or two a photograph of my present possessor – known to Britannia as Miss Menken and to me as Dolores (her real Christian name) – and myself taken together. We both came out very well." I have a print of this interesting carte-de-visite. But the intimate relation did not last much longer, and the Menken left Swinburne and went over to Paris, where she was photographed on the knee of Alexandre Dumas *père* and died on the 10th of August. In talking about Swinburne, she expressed vexation at having failed in the particular mission on which she had been employed, and naïvely remarked to Rossetti "I can't make him understand that biting's no use!" He invariably spoke of her afterwards with admiration and affection, and never hinted at any impediment to their loves. To myself he rather drolly said, in 1875, that her only fault was that she would wake up so early in the morning, and insist on reading her poetry to him. She would swing her handsome legs on the edge of the bed, till he thought they would turn to ice in the cold morning air, but the passion of her poetical rhapsody seemed to keep her warm. This was the first and only liaison in Swinburne's life . . .

It was about this time that he wrote two long poems on flagellation, one in the *Don Juan* stanza, the other in the form of a border ballad. He also wrote a sort of story, in prose, describing a scene. These are entirely without literary merit, except that they could only have been written by Swinburne. I would point out that though all three are very repulsive and monstrous, they are not in any just sense to be described as "bawdy." It is the pain, and the excitement of the nerves caused by enduring pain, and seeing it inflicted, that are dwelt upon, and not any sexual phenomena. I cannot help believing that these scourgings were in some extraordinary way a mode by which the excessive tension of

Swinburne's nerves was relieved. I do not know whether the medical authorities would admit this possibility.

He presently quarrelled, I think about money, with the harpies in St John's Wood, and I have not found any evidence of his going to them after 1869. But his mind continued to turn with fervour to the idea of flagellation, and he was so foolish as to make some very rude designs – for he had not the slightest power of draughtsmanship – of positions and attitudes which he wished some professional artist to carry out for his delectation. The letters to his unworthy agent, who treated him very treacherously, and these rude sketches, fell into the hands of a scoundrel who long afterwards, in the Putney days, used them to blackmail Swinburne. Watts Dunton contrived to buy them back at a high price, which Swinburne had to pay. Apparently, Watts Dunton destroyed the sketches, but, astonishing as it sounds, he carefully preserved the letters, which I was allowed to read after W D's death. I strongly recommended destruction of the letters, which I hope was carried out.

One anecdote connected with the visits to the scourging ladies with the golden hair has a certain literary value. George R Sims told me that in 1868, on mornings when Swinburne was on his way from his lodgings in Dorset Street to the brothel, he used to pause in the Regent's Park, at a particular bench, and write down the verses he had been composing in his head. Several of the *Songs before Sunrise* were so written. Sims was told this fact about his composing these particular poems by a friendly and intelligent park-keeper, who knew who the poet was, and who often conversed with him. There is something very extraordinary in the idea of a man writing these noble and impassioned hymns to the Republic on his way to being whipped at a bawdy-house, but may it not throw a faint light on the physiological cause of the practices which have been described?

1918?

Coventry Patmore

1823–1896

Gosse wrote his biography of Patmore in 1904 and it was published the following year by Hodder and Stoughton in their series "Literary Lives", edited by W Robertson Nicoll. In 1900 Basil Champneys had published two volumes of *Memoirs and Correspondence*. Gosse said in his own preface that that "collection of documents, extremely full and authentic" could never be superseded, but he felt there was room for his own "little volume" to supplement the official biography. He said that "for many years [he] enjoyed the privilege of a close friendship" with Patmore, "and this book, although delayed in publication until now, represents impressions which its author formed during Patmore's life". I am printing most of chapter 6, which Gosse called "Personal Characteristics".

* * *

There can be no question that at the present day too much attention is frequently given to the little acts and oddities of those whose real importance lies entirely in their productions . . . The tendency of modern society is to take away the salient and the surprising elements from the lives of those whose chief mission is an intellectual or a moral one, and there is little that is not trivial or monotonous to record about most of our poets and philosophers. But to this rule every age produces eminent exceptions, and of these Coventry Patmore was one. To deal exclusively with his verses or, as some have wished to do, to soften into mediocrity the violent lines of his personal character, would be to stultify our aim. If we wish to preserve for posterity an opportunity to study this extraordinary man, it is necessary that we should

79

preserve with care the character of his person as well as that of his works. In dwelling faithfully upon what he was, those who observed him closely are not merely justified in setting forth their observations, but have a duty so to do. Patmore himself would have been the first to insist upon this fidelity. He was not one of those who wish the truth to be smothered in foolish posthumous flatteries; he never desired to see the forms of vitality attenuated, but always reinforced. His grim ghost will not rise to upbraid the biographer who strives to paint him exactly as he was.

The central impression which long impact with the mind of Coventry Patmore produced was that here was an example, – possibly the most remarkable example in England at that time, – of the intellectual and moral aristocrat. To no other man of his age was the general trend of the nineteenth century towards uniformity and solidarity so detestable as it was to Patmore. The give and take of modern toleration, the concentrated action of masses of men, whose units fit into one another, meant absolutely nothing to him. He would abandon no privilege for the general convenience; he watched the modern instinct warring against the solitary person, instinctively so hateful to democracies, and he defied it. Defiance was not a burden to him; he was "ever a fighter," requiring for complete mental health the salubrious sensation of antagonism. But even here he was not pleased to face the crowd; he disliked its presence. His notion of fighting was to "fire his ringing shot and pass." He was a militant hermit of the soul, and it was as a hermit-thrush that he poured out his songs – for himself . . .

No one could enter the circle of his conversation without perceiving his pride in a sense of the distance which divided him, and those whom he esteemed, from the crowd, the vast, indefinite *plebs* whom he disdained. His very cordiality, the charming sweetness of his affection, took a lustre from this general hauteur, since the few who were received within the wicket, who were allowed to share the sublime and embattled isolation, were flattered in their inmost nature by so gracious a partiality. He had a very strong sense of inequality. Without anything overtly arrogant, he was irresistibly conscious of a sort of supernatural superiority in himself. He would never have admitted it in words, perhaps because he would expect no sensible person to deny it. He was serene and kindly, but aloof; he was like a king in exile. He had something of the conduct of a dethroned monarch, of one who does not expect homage or wish for it, but who knows that his ideas are sovereign and his claims invulnerable.

His attitude to life, – at all events until the sad reverberation of his last years, – gave a constant impression of accumulated energy, a sense of plenitude. His temper was not parasitical, he did not lean on others or need them; he could stand quite alone. In speaking and in acting he preserved a strong sense of his own value. It was absolutely necessary to his temperament to run his own race, to speak his own thought.

If we study this mental attitude more closely, we find that it denoted the exercise of a singular moral independence. Patmore is not comprehended unless we realize that he deliberately arrogated to himself the right to perform certain intellectual acts which were of an exceptional nature. It appears to me that throughout his whole life in maturity he was training himself to absolute liberty in matters of will, although at the same time, by a paradox which must presently be faced, remaining strictly obedient to the laws of the Church of Rome. This led him to an ingenuity of expression which sometimes appeared casuistical, but there was no real inconsistency. His independence enabled him to believe that he was never driven along paths which seemed those of obedience and renunciation, but that his spirit leaped ahead to obey before the order was given and to renounce in joy before the temptation was formulated. His attitude to certain persons within his own communion showed how anxious he was that his freedom should not be tampered with. The hot flame of the tyrannicide burned in his breast, and he was ready to destroy any one who threatened his individual independence.

In this connexion, nothing is more amusing than his life-long antipathy to Cardinal Manning, in whom, as by an instinct, he perceived the tyrant, the oppressor of others' will. Patmore never faltered for a moment about Manning, whom he described as being "as ignorant as a child in matters of philosophy, although his attitude on such questions was always arrogantly dogmatic." Mr Basil Champneys has given a series of very amusing anecdotes and sayings which betray Patmore's undying hatred of Manning, whom, moreover, he once defined to me as "the worst type in history of the priest-ridden atheist." This, no doubt, was an example of what Mr Champneys excellently calls Patmore's habit of "expressing himself in words which exceeded rather than fell short of his actual sentiments." But it exemplified his passionate and temperamental dislike of Manning, which, without question, was fostered by certain personal incidents connected with Patmore's first and second marriages, but which I believe to have been yet mainly due to a partly unconscious sense of Manning's dangerous and insidious tendency to enslave the human will . . .

The paradox which seems offered to us by the steady and humble faith of a man like Patmore in religious matters, and his extreme self-confidence in everything else, is more apparent than real. Having satisfied himself to the full on the great spiritual question, being troubled by no species of doubt about that, his will was free to exercise itself with the utmost freedom in all mundane directions. If you firmly believe that your volition is melted into God's, there is no difficulty in supposing that if you find yourself wishing for something or approving something, that thing is also approved by God. Patmore made a tremendous effort not to allow the conventions of religion to compromise his will, and, once convinced of the rightness of his central orthodoxy, he had no superstition about the human arrangements of his faith. He was always wide-awake to the dangers of theological charlatanry, and his outspoken remarks on this subject were wont to amuse his friends and to scandalize strangers. In the last letter of his life he referred to Omar Khayyam's disdain of priests with high approval. He took an absolute pleasure in the incongruity between the lofty vocation of these agents of grace and the frailties and defects of their personal conduct.

It is true that, as his closest friend has said, Patmore's "most severe attacks upon the priests were as often as not prompted by a rather mischievous humour which led him to delight in shocking those" who adopted the view that all priests should be regarded as immaculate . . .

*

A certain pessimism in general matters, united to or imposed upon his extraordinary optimism in particular instances, led Patmore to sympathize with those who have despaired of the system of human institutions. He was drawn with a vehement attraction to the dark philosophy of Schopenhauer, of whom he was one of the earliest students in this country. The tremendous effort which Patmore was always making to prevent his religious faith from compromising his intellectual judgment enabled him to tolerate the apparent atheism in the German philosopher's system. But it is very curious to notice that Patmore, like Nietzsche long afterwards (in 1888), recognized in Schopenhauer an element which his general readers were far from observing. Each of them, from his diametrically opposite view, instinctively detected what was still Christian in

Schopenhauer, and observed how much he continued to be domi-
nated by Christian formulas. There is something humorous in
finding an intellectual opinion shared in isolation by Patmore and
– by Nietzsche! But the bellicose element in the former would
probably have found something to sympathize with even in the
violence of the latter.

In the ordinary intercourse of life it was impossible that Patmore
should not be frequently misunderstood by those who did not
appreciate his humour or who had no sense of fun themselves.
He was mischievously contradictory, paradoxical and arbitrary,
and he had a violent hatred for "sentimental faddists, humani-
tarians, anti-tobacconists and teetotalers." Yet he could be
extremely sentimental himself; he was gentle and indulgent to
animals; and few men of his generation indulged more sparingly
in the legitimate stimulus of wine. But in all these movements he
saw an interference with personal freedom of action, a thing for
which he was disposed to fight in the last trench. He was like the
late Archbishop Magee, he would rather see England free than
England sober. He pushed his argument to an extreme: – "The
bank-holidays," he wrote, "are a prodigious nuisance. The whole
population of England seems now to be chronically drunk every
Saturday, Sunday and Monday, Feast-day or Fast. It is very lucky.
Nothing but universal drunkenness among the labouring classes
can keep them from making use, i.e. abuse, of the new political
power. It will be an unhappy day for England when the mechanic
takes to becoming a sober, respectable man." . . .

He had an exaggerated way of saying all things, great and small.
If he heard a blackcap singing in the garden it became at once a
nightingale, and in describing it a few hours later it became "a
chorus of *five* or *six* nightingales." He could not moderate his
praise or blame. Instances of the latter have been given; one of
the former, very characteristic, occurs to me. In the presence of
a number of men of letters, Patmore mentioned an accomplished
writer who was an intimate friend of his. The conversation passed
to the lyrical poems of Herrick, whereupon Patmore, in his most
positive manner, exclaimed, "By the side of − − −, Herrick was
nothing but a brilliant insect!" There was a universal murmur of
indignant protest. Patmore pursed up his lips, blinked his eyes
and said nothing. The conversation proceeded, and an opinion of
Goethe's was presently quoted. Then Patmore lifted up his voice
and cried: – "By the side of − − −, *Goethe* was nothing but a
brilliant insect!" This was an instance of the blind violence of his
humour, perhaps at its worst. It was an attempt to take opinion

83

by storm and to triumph over the bewilderment of his auditors; and truly, in analysing such preposterous utterances, it was often difficult to know how much was conscious fun and how much mere daredevil wilfulness.

His humour often took the form of epigrams or lampoons, by far the most famous of which was that which he wrote in August, 1870, on occasion of the Emperor William's famous telegram from Woerth: –

> This is to say, my dear Augusta,
> We've had another awful buster:
> Ten thousand Frenchmen sent below!
> Thank God from whom all blessings flow.

*

The personal appearance of Coventry Patmore has, most fortunately, been secured for posterity by the art of one of the most gifted of living artists, Mr John S Sargent, RA. Patmore had a great admiration for Mr Sargent's work; he wrote: – "He seems to me to be the greatest, not only of living English portrait painters, but of all English portrait painters." This was certainly a very happy spirit in which to approach the studio, and this enthusiastic appreciation survived the weariness of "sittings." These began in June 1894, and on September 7 Patmore announced the completion of the work as follows: "As you were instrumental in getting the portrait done, I ought to tell you that it is now finished to the satisfaction, and far more than satisfaction, of every one – including the painter – who has seen it. It will be, simply as a work of art, the picture of the Academy," where, indeed, in 1895, it attracted universal admiration. In the same month of September 1894, Mr Sargent, saying that he had only done half of Patmore as yet, painted a second portrait, and later on the poet came up to town to sit for the Prophet Ezekiel in that great decorative composition which Mr Sargent was painting for the Boston Library. There are, therefore, three portraits – the most important of them already transferred to the National Portrait Gallery – in which a hand of consummate power has fixed for ever upon canvas the apocalyptical old age of Coventry Patmore.

Splendid as these portraits are, however, and intimately true of the poet's latest phase, it is necessary to insist that he was not always thus ragged and vulturine, not always such a miraculous portent of gnarled mandible and shaken plumage . . . When I saw him first in 1879, [his salient characteristics] were still far from giving him that aspect of a wild crane in the wilderness which Mr Sargent's marvellous portrait will pass down to posterity. He was exceedingly unlike other people, of course, even then, but his face possessed quite as much beauty as strangeness. Three things were in those days particularly noticeable in the head of Coventry Patmore: the vast convex brows, arched with vision; the bright, shrewd, bluish-grey eyes, the outer fold of one eyelid permanently and humorously drooping; and the wilful, sensuous mouth. These three seemed ever at war among themselves; they spoke three different tongues; they proclaimed a man of dreams, a canny man of business, a man of vehement physical determination. It was the harmony of these in apparently discordant contrast which made the face so fascinating; the dwellers under this strange mask were three, and the problem was how they contrived the common life. The same incongruity pervaded all the poet's figure. When at rest, standing or sitting, he was remarkably graceful, falling easily into languid, undulating poses. No sooner did he begin to walk than he became grotesque at once, the long, thin neck thrust out, the angularity of the limbs emphasized in every rapid, inelegant movement. Sailing along the Parade at Hastings, his hands deep in the pockets of his short, black-velvet jacket, his grey curls escaping from under a broad, soft wide-awake hat, his long, thin legs like compasses measuring the miles, his fancy manifestly "reaching to some great world in ungauged darkness hid," Coventry Patmore was an apparition never to be forgotten.

His relations with others partook of the incongruity which I have tried to note in his personal appearance. On one side, Patmore was sociable up to the very last, pleased to meet strangers, to feel the movement of young persons circling around him; on another, he was averse to companionship, a solitary, a hermit. He loved the society of the ladies of his family, but he was something of a Pacha even there. They were not expected to disturb his day dream, and sometimes he brusquely shook them off him. Then he would write to some male friend: "It would be a charity if you would come down now and then on Saturday and stay till Monday. I live all my days in a wilderness of fair women, and I long for some male chat." Or, in these moods, he would break away altogether and come up to town, descending suddenly on some active friend, who would be always delighted, of course, to see him, but embarrassed, in the hurly-burly of business, to know what to do with this grim pilgrim who would sit there for hours, winking, blinking, smoking innumerable cigarettes, and saying next to nothing. Little parties suddenly collected to meet Patmore at luncheon or dinner were found to be the most successful form of entertainment; for though he would sometimes scarcely say a word, or would wither conversation by some paradox ending in a crackle and a cough, it was discovered that he believed himself to have been almost indecorously sparkling on these occasions, and would long afterwards refer to a very dull, small dinner as "that fearful dissipation."

He was so very loyal to his restricted friendships, that a fresh incongruity is to be traced in the notorious fact that he had sacrificed more illustrious friends on the altar of caprice than any other man in England. He had been intimate with Tennyson, Emerson, Browning, Rossetti, Millais, and Woolner, yet each of these intimacies ceased as time went on, and each was broken off or dropped by Patmore. He got a reputation in some quarters for churlishness, which it is not very easy to explain away, yet which he did not quite deserve. The cessation of these relationships was due to several causes. In the cases of Tennyson, and in lesser measure of Ruskin, the youthful spirit of idolatry had given place to a mature independence not so agreeable to the idol. In some of these instances, when the tie had become irksome, it was snapped by what was called a "quarrel," an incident often of highly mysterious character. Every one who knew Patmore well has heard him tell the story of his "quarrel" with Tennyson. I was at pains to sift this anecdote, and was able to prove to my own satisfaction that it could not have happened. It was simply, I think, a casuistical mode of freeing Patmore's memory from the burden of Tennyson's influence. In this connexion, as Patmore's absence from Tennyson's funeral has been commented on, I am glad to take this opportunity of explaining it. Patmore was so anxious to be present that he came to London for the purpose, without waiting for the indispensable card of invitation. This latter was sent to Hastings by mistake, and thence to Lymington, and thence to town, reaching Patmore an hour after the ceremony began in the Abbey. Two years before Tennyson's death, the old friends exchanged kindly verbal greetings through a third person, but neither would write first to the other, and they met no more.

Another cause for the rupture of certain early friendships was religious sentiment. It must never be forgotten that Patmore was not merely a Catholic, but an enthusiastically convinced and strenuous one. His conversion to Rome severed many old ties, and he was not anxious that these should be renewed. His attitude to Rossetti was typical. He spoke of no one with more heat of resentment than of Rossetti; I remember that, on occasion of that poet's death, in 1882, I was bewildered by Patmore's expressions. He drew himself up in his chair, his eyes blazed, he was like the Prophet Ezekiel in his denunciation. He considered, so he explained, that Rossetti, more than any other man since the great old artist-age, had been dowered with insight into spiritual mysteries, that the Ark of passion had been delivered into his hands and that he had played with it, had used it to serve his curiosity and his vanity, had profaned the Holy of Holies; that he was Uzzah and Pandarus, and that there was no forgiveness for him anywhere. And even Ruskin, though in lesser degree, and with far less seriousness, for the affection here lasted warmly to the end, came in at times for fantastic denunciation. In these sallies, fun and earnest were indissolubly mixed, yet it was very far indeed from being all fun.

Patmore's austerity being, as it was, strongly emphasized by his candour of speech and virile intellectual independence, it is well to note that he was by no means, at least in the Puritan sense, ascetic . . . He once said to me, "No one is thoroughly convinced of the truth of his religion who is afraid to joke about it, just as no man can tease a woman with such impunity as he who is perfectly convinced of her love." He did not scruple to invent Catholic legends, some of which are now, we are told, in steady circulation among the devout. In particular, I remember a story about the dormouse, who was created with a naked tail like a rat, but who, seeing Adam and Eve eating the apple, and being conscious of a sinful longing, pressed what tail he had to his eyes to shut out temptation. He was instantly rewarded by the not very silky brush which has been the pride of his descendants. This Patmore invented, circulated, and had the exquisite pleasure, – so, at least, he affirmed, – of seeing adopted into works of Catholic tradition.

It is entertaining to those who knew Coventry Patmore well to hear him conjectured of by those who never saw him as "mild" or "namby-pamby." In point of fact, he was the most masterful of men, the very type of that lofty, moral arrogance which antiquity identified with the thought of Archilochus. This partly essential, partly exterior tendency to tyrannize, to be a law to himself and others, to cut all knots whatsoever with a single, final slash of that stringent tongue of his, was, indeed, a snare to him. It obscured too often the sunshine of his sensitive tenderness, and in such poems as "The Toys" and "If I were Dead" a piteous proof is offered to us that he was conscious of this. His hand was apt to be too heavy in reproof; what to himself seemed tempered

87

by its humorous exaggeration fell upon the culprit with a crushing weight. And then Patmore would be sorry for his anger, and angry with himself for being sorry, until the fountains that should have been sweet and clear were bitter and turbid with conflicting emotion.

Rarely has a knowledge of the man been more essential to the comprehension of his writings than was the case with Coventry Patmore. To understand the poems, some vision of the angular, vivid, discordant, and yet exquisitely fascinating person who composed them is necessary. During a great portion of his life, the genius of Patmore was under an almost unbroken cloud; it was the object of ridicule and rebuke; even now, when honour is generally paid to his name, the extraordinary originality and force of his best work is properly appreciated by but few. It is my firm conviction that the influence of Coventry Patmore, as the master-psychologist of love, human and divine, is destined steadily to increase, and that a future generation will look back to him with a mingled homage and curiosity when many of those whose doings now fill the columns of our newspapers are forgotten. For, in this composite age of ours, when all things and people are apt to seem repetitions of people and things which amused some previous generation, Coventry Patmore contrived, unconsciously, to give the impression of being, like the Phœnix of fable, the solitary specimen of an unrelated species.

1904.

Walt Whitman
1819–1892

Gosse's account of his visit to Whitman was published in *Critical Kit-Kats*. It first appeared in the *New Review* in April 1894, nearly ten years after the visit. The circumstances of the visit are examined in the notes on this essay. Gosse wrote to Whitman from New York on 29 December 1884: "I am very anxious not to leave this country without paying my respects to you, and bearing to you in person the messages which I bring from Mr Swinburne and other common friends. I propose therefore if it be not inconvenient to you, to call upon you in Camden on Saturday next, in the forenoon." Whitman replied that he would be glad to see him: "I live less than half a mile from the ferry landing here."

Gosse's diary entry for 3rd January 1885 reads simply:

By the ferry over to Camden. Walt Whitman's modest little house (W Whitman on the plate). Hobbled half way down stairs. Uncarpeted room with bright outlook on to the street. Stove which he constantly attended to. Long white hair, open shirt, broad white hat lying around. Genial manner. "My friend." Spoke of Swinburne & Tennyson. Most kind. Head from behind like Darwin. Brought a book. He read me a new poem, intoning it, not very distinctly. Miss Smith & her friend, Boston enthusiasts, came in. Whitman consulting us about a preface & a portrait. He talked of his "barbaric yawp" smilingly. Great sense of "the calm within, the light around, & that content, etc." The boys, lovely days when he was young, & about with "the boys" in the sun. Bathes now, and lies in the sun, in a NJ brooklet in summer. Love of the sun. Portrait of Harlan. Likes to walk about in Philadelphia.

Whitman's friend, William Douglas O'Connor, wrote to Whitman on 1 February 1885: "Gosse's visit to you, and his kind and respectful words, inexpressibly gratified me. What gave it all point was that he had been feted to the very top of the literacy and aristocracy everywhere in the country." Whitman was not so impressed. He said to his friend Horace Traubel that O'Connor seemed to think Gosse's visit so significant. "I do not know about the significance," Whitman replied – "I was glad to hear from him, glad to have him come. Gosse is very largely a formal craftsman", (Whitman was obviously thinking of his poems), "but he has a little disposition our way." On 25 May 1888 Traubel noted Whitman saying "There was Gosse too: he was originally on my side – very warm (almost effervescent) – he, too, they tell me, though so new, has weakened just a bit." Gosse was nervous of identifying too closely with Whitman because of the strong homosexual tone of his work, which had appealed so much to Gosse at one stage in his life.

In a piece on Whitman in the *Sunday Times*, which eventually appeared in his last collection, *Leaves and Fruit* (1927), Gosse sums up his feelings about the poet who had then been dead for 35 years:

> There is one author who has the peculiarity of being attractive or repulsive to the same persons at different periods of life, or condition, or even weather ... It depends not so much on him as on themselves; on whether they are young and eager or weary of life ...

It says much for Gosse that at the very end of his life he could end his essay, after some reference to Whitman's love for men and the "subterfuge of his alarmed correspondence with John Addington Symonds":

> It is best not to inquire too closely about all this, but to accept Walt Whitman for what he gives, for his prodigious candour, his zest in life, his "sweet aromatic presence", the undeniable beauty and originality of his strange unshackled rhapsody.

* * *

In the early and middle years of his life, Whitman was obscure and rarely visited. When he grew old, pilgrims not unfrequently took scrip and staff, and set out to worship him. Several accounts of his appearance and mode of address on these occasions have been published, and if I add one more it must be my excuse that the visit to be described was not undertaken in the customary spirit. All other accounts, so far as I know, of interviews with Whitman have been written by disciples who approached the shrine adoring and ready to be dazzled. The visitor whose experience – and it was a very delightful one – is now to be chronicled, started under what was, perhaps, the disadvantage of being very unwilling to go; at least, it will be admitted that the tribute – for tribute it has to be – is all the more sincere.

When I was in Boston, in the winter of 1884, I received a note from Whitman asking me not to leave America without coming to see him. My first instinct was promptly to decline the invitation. Camden, New Jersey, was a very long way off. But better counsels prevailed; curiosity and civility combined to draw me, and I wrote to him that I would come. It would be fatuous to mention all this, if it were not that I particularly wish to bring out the peculiar magic of the old man, acting, not on a disciple, but on a stiff-necked and froward unbeliever.

To reach Camden, one must arrive at Philadelphia, where I put up on the 2nd of January, 1885, ready to pass over into New Jersey next morning. I took the hall-porter of the hotel into my confidence, and asked if he had ever heard of Mr Whitman. Oh, yes, they all knew "Walt," he said; on fine days he used to cross over on the ferry and take the tram into Philadelphia. He liked to stroll about in Chestnut Street and look at the people, and if you smiled at him he would smile back again; everybody knew "Walt." In the North, I had been told that he was almost bedridden, in consequence of an attack of paralysis. This seemed inconsistent with wandering around Philadelphia.

The distance being considerable, I started early on the 3rd, crossed the broad Delaware River, where blocks of ice bumped and crackled around us, and saw the flat shores of New Jersey expanding in front, raked by the broad morning light. I was put ashore in a crude and apparently uninhabited village, grim with that concentrated ugliness that only an American township in the depth of winter can display. Nobody to ask the way, or next to nobody. I wandered aimlessly about, and was just ready to give all I possessed to be back again in New York, when I discovered that I was opposite No. 328 Mickle Street, and that on a minute brass plate was engraved "W Whitman." I knocked at this dreary little two-storey tenement house, and wondered what was going to happen. A melancholy woman opened the door; it was too late now to go away. But before I could speak, a large figure, hobbling down the stairs, called out in a cheery voice, "Is that my friend?" Suddenly, by I know not what magnetic charm, all wire-drawn literary reservations faded out of being, and one's only sensation was of gratified satisfaction at being the "friend" of this very nice old gentleman.

There was a good deal of greeting on the stairs, and then the host, moving actively, though clumsily, and with a stick, advanced to his own dwelling-room on the first storey. The opening impression was, as the closing one would be, of extreme simplicity.

A large room, without carpet on the scrubbed planks, a small bedstead, a little round stove with a stack-pipe in the middle of the room, one chair – that was all the furniture. On the walls and in the fireplace such a miserable wall-paper – tinted, with a spot – as one sees in the bedrooms of labourers' cottages; no pictures hung in the room, but pegs and shelves loaded with objects. Various boxes lay about, and one huge clamped trunk, and heaps, mountains of papers in a wild confusion, swept up here and there into stacks and peaks; but all the room, and the old man himself, clean in the highest degree, raised to the nth power of stainlessness, scoured and scrubbed to such a pitch that dirt seemed defied for all remaining time. Whitman, in particular, in his suit of hodden grey and shirt thrown wide open at the throat, his grey hair and whiter beard voluminously flowing, seemed positively blanched with cleanliness; the whole man sand-white with spotlessness, like a deal table that has grown old under the scrubbing-brush.

Whitman sat down in the one chair with a small poker in his hand and spent much of his leisure in feeding and irritating the stove. I cleared some papers away from off a box and sat opposite to him. When he was not actively engaged upon the stove his steady attention was fixed upon his visitor, and I had a perfect opportunity of forming a mental picture of him. He sat with a very curious pose of the head thrown backward, as if resting it one vertebra lower down the spinal column than other people do, and thus tilting his face a little upwards. With his head so poised and the whole man fixed in contemplation of the interlocutor, he seemed to pass into a state of absolute passivity, waiting for remarks or incidents, the glassy eyes half closed, the large knotted hands spread out before him. So he would remain, immovable for a quarter of an hour at a time, even the action of speech betraying no movement, the lips hidden under a cascade of beard. If it be true that all remarkable human beings resemble animals, then Walt Whitman was like a cat – a great old grey Angora Tom, alert in repose, serenely blinking under his combed waves of hair, with eyes inscrutably dreaming.

His talk was elemental, like his writings. It had none of the usual ornaments or irritants of conversation. It welled out naturally, or stopped; it was innocent of every species of rhetoric or epigram. It was the perfectly simple utterance of unaffected urbanity. So, I imagine, an Oriental sage would talk, in a low uniform tone, without any excitement or haste, without emphasis, in a land where time and flurry were unknown. Whitman sat there with his great head tilted back, smiling serenely, and he talked about himself. He mentioned his poverty, which was patent, and his paralysis; those were the two burdens beneath which he crouched, like Issachar; he seemed to be quite at home with both of them, and scarcely heeded them. I think I asked leave to move my box, for the light began to pour in at the great uncurtained window; and then Whitman said that some one had promised him a gift of curtains, but he was not eager for them, he thought they "kept out some of the light." Light and air, that was all he wanted; and through the winter he sat there patiently waiting for the air and light of summer, when he would hobble out again and bask his body in a shallow creek he knew "back of Camden." Meanwhile he waited, waited with infinite patience, uncomplaining, thinking about the sand, and the thin hot layer of water over it, in that shy New Jersey creek. And he winked away in silence, while I thought of the Indian poet Valmiki, when, in a trance of voluptuous abstraction, he sat under the fig-tree and was slowly eaten of ants.

In the bareness of Whitman's great double room only two objects suggested art in any way, but each of these was appropriate. One was a print of a Red Indian, given him, he told me, by Catlin; it had inspired the passage about "the red aborigines" in *Starting from Paumanok*. The other – positively the sole and only thing that redeemed the bareness of the back-room where Whitman's bound works were stored – was a photograph of a very handsome young man in a boat, sculling. I asked him about this portrait and he said several notable things in consequence. He explained, first of all, that this was one of his greatest friends, a professional oarsman from Canada, a well-known sporting character. He continued, that these were the people he liked best, athletes who had a business in the open air; that those were the plainest and most affectionate of men, those who lived in the light and air and had to study to keep their bodies clean and fresh and ruddy; that his soul went out to such people, and that they were strangely drawn to him, so that at the lowest ebb of his fortunes, when the world reviled him and ridiculed him most, fortunate men of this kind, highly prosperous as gymnasts or runners, had sought him out and had been friendly to him. "And now," he went on, "I only wait for the spring, to hobble out with my staff into the woods, and when I can sit all day long close to a set of woodmen at their work, I am perfectly happy, for something of their life mixes with the smell of the chopped timber, and it passes into my veins and I am old and ill no longer." I think these were

93

his precise words, and they struck me more than anything else that he said throughout that long and pleasant day I spent with him.

It might be supposed, and I think that even admirers have said, that Whitman had no humour. But that seemed to me not quite correct. No boisterous humour, truly, but a gentle sort of sly fun, something like Tennyson's, he certainly showed. For example, he told me of some tribute from India, and added, with a twinkling smile, "You see, I 'sound my barbaric yawp over the roofs of the world.' " But this was rare: mostly he seemed dwelling in a vague pastoral past life, the lovely days when he was young, and went about with "the boys" in the sun. He read me many things; a new "poem," intoning the long irregular lines of it not very distinctly; and a preface to some new edition. All this has left, I confess, a dim impression, swallowed up in the serene self-unconsciousness, the sweet, dignified urbanity, the feline immobility.

As I passed from the little house and stood in dull, deserted Mickle Street once more, my heart was full of affection for this beautiful old man, who had just said in his calm accents, "Goodbye, my friend!" I felt that the experience of the day was embalmed by something that a great poet had written long ago, but I could not find what it was till we started once more to cross the frosty Delaware; then it came to me, and I knew that when Shelley spoke of

> Peace within and calm around,
> And that content, surpassing wealth,
> The sage in meditation found,
> And walk'd with inward glory crown'd,

he had been prophesying of Walt Whitman, nor shall I ever read those lines again without thinking of the old rhapsodist in his empty room, glorified by patience and philosophy.

And so an unbeliever went to see Walt Whitman, and was captivated without being converted . . .

1893.

Wolcott Balestier

1861–1891

This portrait first appeared in the April 1892 issue of the *Century* and was then privately printed in an edition of 100 copies. It was reprinted in *Portraits and Sketches* 20 years later. Gosse saw himself as a vital player in Balestier's life in England and claimed credit for having introduced him to Rudyard Kipling, who became his co-author and married his sister Caroline after Balestier's death.

Gosse was overwhelmed by Balestier's early death – that was his own word at the time. He wrote to one of his American friends, Richard Watson Gilder: "I know not how to get on without him – without his sympathy, his energy, his encouragement". Henry James was also devastated by his death and indeed chided Gosse for his unflattering remarks about Balestier's appearance and his secretiveness. "To the young, the early dead, the baffled, the defeated, I don't think we can be tender enough," James wrote, though Gosse had written with considerable warmth and sensitivity. It was 20 years later that Gosse betrayed both his own earlier feelings and Balestier himself by writing to George Douglas: "You would have detested him. I should have detested him, but that he happened to like me very much. He was a queer, strained tight little type of strenuous Yankee: not important, not (perhaps) worthy of a place in the gallery, but curious and original in his common and imitative way!" In spite of these unattractive second thoughts (which certainly contradict the impression Balestier left on J H Shorthouse, for instance: "so refined and delicate in its charm"), Gosse's portrait of Balestier seems worth a place in this gallery.

*   *   *

It was early in 1889 that, on an evening which must always remain memorable to some of us, two or three English writers met, at

95

the house of Mrs Humphry Ward, a young American man of business who had just made her acquaintance. Among those who then saw Wolcott Balestier for the first time were Mr Henry James (soon to become his closest and most valued friend in England) and the writer of these pages. As I look back upon that evening, and ask myself what it was in the eager face I watched across the table-cloth which could create so instant a thrill of attraction, so unresisted a prescience of an intimate friendship ready to invade me, I can hardly find an answer. The type was not of that warm and sympathetic class so familiar in our race; neither in colour, form, nor character was it English. In later moments one analyzed that type – a mixture of the suave colonial French and the strained, nervous New England blood. But, at first sight, a newly presented acquaintance gained an impression of Wolcott Balestier as a carefully dressed young-old man or elderly youth, clean-shaven, with smooth dark hair, thin nose, large sensitive ears, and whimsically mobile mouth. The singular points in this general appearance, however, were given by the extreme pallor of the complexion and by the fire in the deeply-set dark blue eyes; for the rest, a spare and stooping figure, atonic, ungraceful, a general physique ill-matched with the vigour of will, the extreme rapidity of graceful mental motion, the protean variety and charm of intellectual vitality, that inhabited this frail bodily dwelling. To the very last, after seeing him almost daily for nearly three years, I never could entirely lose the sense of the capricious contrast between this wonderful intelligence and the unhelpful frame that did it so much wrong.

Charles Wolcott Balestier had just entered his twenty-eighth year when first I knew him. He was born at Rochester, New York, on December 13, 1861. His paternal great-grandfather had been a French planter in the island of Martinique; his maternal grandfather, whom he is said to have physically resembled, was a jurist who completed commercial negotiations between the United States and Japan. Of his early life I know but little. Wolcott Balestier was at school in his native city, and at college for a short time at Cornell University, but his education was, I suppose, mainly that of life itself. After his boyhood he spent a few years on the outskirts of literature. I learn from Mr W D Howells that at the age of seventeen he began to send little tales and essays to the office of the *Atlantic Monthly*. He edited a newspaper, later on, in Rochester; he published in succession three short novels; and he was employed in the Astor Library in New York.

All these incidents, however, have little significance. But in the

winter of 1882 he made an excursion to Leadville, which pro-
foundly impressed his imagination. The Colorado air was more
than his weak chest could endure, and he soon came back; but
two years later he made a second trip to the West, in company
with his elder sister, and this lasted for many months. He returned,
at length, through Mexico and the Southern States. The glimpses
that he gained in 1885 of the fantastic life of the West remained
to the end of his career the most vivid and exciting which his
memory retained. The desire to write earnestly seized him, and
it was in Colorado that the first crude sketch of the book afterwards re-written as "Benefits Forgot" was composed. Soon after
his return to New York he became known to and highly appreciated by men in business, and in the winter of 1888 he came over
to England to represent a New York publisher and to open an
office in London.

Of his three full years in the latter city I can speak with some
authority, for I was in close relation with him during the greater
part of that time. He arrived in England without possessing the
acquaintance of a single Englishman, and he died leaving behind
him a wider circle of literary friends than, probably, any other
living American possessed. He had an ardent desire to form personal connections with those whose writings in any way interested
him – to have his finger, as he used to say, on the pulse of
literature – and the peculiarity of his position in London, as the
representative of an American publishing-house, not merely facili-
tated the carrying out of this ambition, but turned that pleasure
into a duty. He possessed a singularly winning mode of address
with strangers whose attention he wished to gain. It might be
described as combining the extreme of sympathetic resignation
with the self-respect needful to make that resignation valuable. It
was in the nature of the business in which Balestier was occupied
during his stay in England that novels (prose fiction in all its
forms) should take up most of his thoughts. I believe that there
was not one English novelist, from George Meredith and Mr
Thomas Hardy down to the most obscure and "subterranean"
writer of popular tales, with whom he did not come into relations
of one sort or another, but sympathetic and courteous in every
case. He was able to preserve in a very remarkable degree his
fine native taste in literature, while conscientiously and eagerly
"trading" for his friends in New York in literary goods which were
not literature at all. This balance of his mind constantly amazed
me. His lofty standard of literary merit was never lowered; it
grew, if anything, more exacting; yet no touch of priggishness, of

97

disdain, coloured his intercourse with those who produce what the public buys in defiance of taste, the honest purveyors of deciduous fiction.

Balestier's ambition on landing, an obscure youth, in an England which had never heard of him was no less than to conquer a place of influence in the centre of English literary society. Within three years he had positively succeeded in gaining such a position, and was daily strengthening it. There has been no such recent invasion of London; he was not merely, as we used to tell him, "one of our conquerors," but the most successful of them all.

What was so novel and so delightful in his relations with authors was the exquisite adroitness with which he made his approaches. He never lost a shy conquest through awkwardness or roughness. If an anthology of appreciations of Wolcott Balestier could be formed, it would show that to each literary man and woman whom he visited he displayed a tincture of his or her own native colour. Soon after his death I received a letter from the author of *John Inglesant*, to whom in the winter of 1890 I had given Balestier a letter of introduction. "The impression he left upon me," says Mr Shorthouse, "was so refined and delicate in its charm that I looked back to it all through that terrible winter with a bright recollection of what is to me the most delightful of experiences, a quiet dinner with a sympathetic and intelligent man."

Our notices of the dead tend to grow stereotyped and featureless. We attribute to them all the virtues, all the talents, but shrink from the task of discrimination. But the sketch which should dwell on Wolcott Balestier mainly as on an amiable young novelist cut off in the flower of his literary youth would fail more notably than usual in giving an impression of the man. Of his literary work I shall presently speak: to praise it with exaggeration would, as I shall try to show, be unwise. But all men are not mere machines for writing boks, and Balestier, pre-eminently, was not. The character was far more unique, more curious, than the mere talent for composition, and what the character was I must now try to describe. He had, in the first place, a business capacity which in its degree may not be very rare, if we regard the whole industrial field, but which as directed to the profession of publication was, I am not afraid to say, unique. He glanced over the field of the publishing-houses, and saw them all divided in interests, pulling various ways, impeding one another, sacrificing the author to their traditions and their lack of enterprise.

Balestier dreamed great dreams of consolidation, at which those who are incapable of the effort of dreaming may now smile, if they will. But no one who is acquainted with details to which I must not do more than allude here will deny that he possessed many of the characteristics needed to turn his dreams into facts. He held in his grasp the details of the trade, yet combined with them an astonishing power of generalisation. I have never known any one connected with the art or trade of literature who had anything like his power of marshalling before his memory, in due order, all the militant English writers of the moment, small as well as great. There they stood in seemly rows, the names that every Englishman honours and never buys, the names that every Englishman buys and never honours. Balestier knew them all, knew their current value, appraised them for future quotation, keeping his own critical judgment, all the while, unbent, but steadily suspended.

To reach this condition of experience time, of course, had been required, but really very little. Within twelve months he knew the English book-market as, probably, no Englishman knew it. Into this business of his he threw an indomitable will, infinite patience, a curious hunting or sporting zest, and what may be called the industrial imagination. His mind moved with extreme rapidity; he never seemed to require to be told a fact or given a hint twice. When you saw him a few days later the fact had gathered to itself a cluster of associate supports, the hint had already ripened to action. I may quote an instance which has a pathetic interest now. In the autumn of 1889, fresh from reading "Soldiers Three," I told him that he ought to keep his eye on a new Indian writer, Rudyard Kipling. "Rudyard Kipling?" he answered impatiently; "is it a man or a woman? What's its real name?" A little nettled, I said, "You will find that you won't be allowed to go on asking questions like those. He is going to be one of the greatest writers of the day." "Pooh, pooh!" Balestier replied, "now you are shouting!" And no further reference was made to the subject. But three days later I found a pile of the blue Indian pamphlets on his desk, and within a week he had added the future collaborator in "The Naulahka" to the troop of what he used to call his "personal conquests."

No striking qualities, as we know, are without their defects. The most trying peculiarity of Wolcott Balestier was the result of his rapidity in decisive manoeuvring. He had cultivated such a perfect gift for being all things to all men, discretion and tact were so requisite in his calling, that he fell, and that increasingly, into the error of excessive reticence. This mysterious secrecy, which grew on him towards the last, his profound caution and subtlety, would doubtless have become modified; this feature of his character needed but to become a little exaggerated, and he would himself have perceived and corrected it. There was perhaps a little temptation to vanity in the case of a young man possessed of so many secrets, and convinced of his worth as a confidential adviser. He "had the unfortunate habit of staring very hard at his own actions, and when he found his relations to others refining themselves under a calcium light, he endeavoured to put up the screen." These words from a story of his own may be twisted into an application that he never intended. In the light of his absolute and unshaken discretion, of his ardent loyalty to his particular friends, of his zeal for the welfare of others, this little tortuous foible for mystery dwindles into something almost too small to be recorded.

For the ordinary relaxations of mankind, especially for the barbarous entertainments of us red-blooded islanders, he had an amused and tolerant disdain. He rode a little, but he had no care for any other sort of exercise. He played no games, he followed no species of sport. His whole soul burned in his enterprises, in his vast industrial dreams. If he tried golf, it was because he was fond of Mr Norris; if he discussed agriculture and Wessex, it was because that was the way to the heart of Mr Thomas Hardy. Nothing came amiss to him in conversation, and he was so apt a learner that he would talk charmingly of politics, of wine, of history, even of the fine arts. But only three things really occupied his mind – the picturesque procession of the democratic life of to-day, the features and fortunes of his friends, and those commercial adventures for the conduct of which he had so extraordinary a genius.

It is by design that I have not spoken hitherto of his own literary productions. It would be easier, I think, to exaggerate their positive value than to overrate the value of the man who wrote them. The three novels which he published in America (*A Patent Philtre*, 1884; *A Fair Device*, 1884; *A Victorious Defeat*, 1886) were the outcome of an admiration for the later novels of Mr W D Howells, but they had not the merit even of being good imitations. Balestier was conscious of their weakness, and he deliberately set himself to forget them. Meanwhile the large issues of life in the West and its social peculiarities fascinated him. The result of his study of the Leadville of 1885 will be found in a novel called "Benefits Forgot," which was finished in 1890, and published in 1892. During the last year of his life Wolcott Balestier took to composition again with much fervour and assiduity. There is no question that his intimate friendship with so eager and brilliant a writer of tales as Mr Rudyard Kipling, who, as is known, became his brother-in-law, was of vast service to him. The short stories of his last year showed a remarkable advance. There remains the part of *The Naulahka* which he contributed, but on this it is impossible here to dwell. What he might have done, if he had lived ten years longer, none of us can conjecture.

The melancholy task remains to me of telling how so much of light and fire was extinguished. He habitually overworked himself to such a degree, the visible mental strain was so obvious, that his health had long given us the deepest anxiety. I, for one, for a year had almost ceased to hope that he could survive. Yet it now appears, both from the record of his family and from the opinion of the German doctors, that there was no organic mischief, and that he might, in spite of his weakness, have lived to old age. He was overworked, but he never worried; he was exhausted, but he did not experience the curse of sleeplessness. In November, however, after some days of indisposition, looking all the while extremely ill, he left London for business reasons, and went to Berlin. We heard of him a few days later as laid up in Dresden. His mother and sisters immediately went to him from Paris. The disease proved to be typhoid fever in a most malignant form, and on the twenty-first day, Sunday, December 6, 1891, he died, having not quite completed his thirtieth year. He lies buried in the American cemetery at Dresden, and our anticipations lie with him:

> For what was he? Some novel power
>   Sprang up for ever at a touch,
>   And hope could never hope too much
> In watching him from hour to hour.

1892.

Thomas Hardy

1840–1928

Gosse never attempted a full-scale portrait of Hardy, but his account of his visit to Max Gate in 1912, which is at Princeton and has apparently never been published, gives a vivid impression of the great writer towards the end of their long friendship. Sixteen years earlier, in 1896, Gosse had dedicated *Critical Kit-Kats*, from which three of the portraits in this new book are taken, to "My Dear Hardy". He recalled a time when, "many years ago" (it was actually 1886) the two friends had lost their way in Bridport and had been misdirected by a young man when they asked the way to the station. Bridport remained with them a symbol for misleading criticism, and Gosse hoped that his collection might not be "of the Bridport order". "What if every judgment in it but misleads and misdirects?" He suggests that Hardy should take the book, "for the sake of the comrade, not of the critic. Take it as a land mark in that friendship, to me inestimably precious, which has now lasted more than twenty years, and will continue, I hope and think, unbroken till one or other of us can enter into no further earthly relations."

Thomas Hardy wrote his last letter to Edmund Gosse on Christmas Day, 1927, in response to Gosse's praise of Hardy's poem "Christmas in the Elgin Room", which had appeared in the *Times* the day before. It was the last letter Hardy wrote. He died 17 days later, on Wednesday, 11 January 1928. Gosse was one of the pall-bearers at the funeral in Westminster Abbey.

Gosse was 78 but he was still contributing regularly to the *Sunday Times* and on 15 January his tribute to his old friend appeared under the headings A VACANT THRONE. THE WRITER AND THE MAN. Soon after this obituary appeared, Gosse expanded his tribute in a broadcast which survives in various forms. In 1950 Ronald Knight bought "a set of two 78rpm gramophone records, published by Columbia Records on behalf of the International Educational Society". According to him, the original discs were cut on 29 March 1928. In 1968,

103

Knight published a rather inaccurate transcription of the broadcast with an introduction by Lois Deacon. The brief *Sunday Times* version, given here, sums up Gosse's feelings about Hardy. It should be read, if possible, hearing in one's mind the eloquence of a fine Victorian actor, mannered and formal but also splendid and totally sincere. Shortly after he had made the broadcast, Gosse was himself no longer capable of entering into "further earthly relations".

* * *

A VISIT TO THOMAS HARDY IN 1912

Today, I took Arthur Benson in his motor to visit Thomas Hardy. A dark cold morning, with a shrewd wind that reddened our faces. We passed rapidly through the heart of Wessex, the province to which a little man of great genius has given a strong spiritual life. A stunted, frightened, reserved yeoman, autochthonous, sprung from the soil, rooted to the soil, has found the secret of this undulating boskage, these rounded bastions of turf, these ancient clusters of grey masonry. He has given them a conscious life, a fresh meaning, while preserving the mystery of their age. We whirled along, through the rising and falling of the ashen colour, the lush double emerald of turf and foliage. We flew through Cerne Abbas, and the Chalk Man, strongly drawn on the hill-side, naked, unabashed, the Man that Caesar saw as we see him, leaned above us in his colossal nudity, symbol of the fertile earth, of dim inconceivable horrors of primal worship. Through Dorchester we race, Dorchester with its prettiness, its dapper air, thrown like a modern dress over the ancient force of its members. As we approach Max Gate, all semblance of age ceases; here is the twentieth century unashamed, its railway-lines, its mean useful buildings, its painful vision of the new Benthamism, cheap and tame and commonplace.

Max Gate, itself, which I saw quite new and bare twenty-five years ago, is utterly changed. All round it, a gross growth of underwood has pushed up, and drowned it. In the dark September air, there was something almost sinister in its overrichness; all this pale vegetation, sprouting too rapidly in the soft Dorset air, seems to suck out of the ground an atmosphere hostile to the human lungs. We left the motor outside, and penetrated under a low ceiling of branches, elms and chestnuts and sycamores crowded too closely together. The little house, absurd with its blunt tower, has an air of insufficiency, as if built too rapidly by a man seized by the fear of finding himself without a shelter, built in disregard of the future, from exiguous resources, not slowly and amorously lifted into existence by one who had time to reflect and a purpose in the future.

We are received, as though unexpected, by a bewildered maid. In the drawing-room, a pleasant, slovenly place crowded with incongruous objects, Emma Hardy greets us with effusion, absurdly dressed, as a country lady without friends might dress herself on a vague recollection of some nymph in a picture by Botticelli. So long we waited, that I remonstrated, "But Tom expects us?" "Oh yes, he has been talking about your visit all the morning." At last the great man appears, grown, it seems to me, very small, very dry, very white. He greets me with a tempered affection, Benson with a reserved graciousness. His eyes are smaller than ever, drawn with fatigue down deeper between the thin, pencilled eyelids. The hair has almost wholly worn away from the forehead, the moustache, once yellowish red, has faded into pallor, it is like the sparse whiskers of some ancient rodent, a worn-out squirrel for instance. The almond shape of the head, rapidly arching above, and as rapidly arching to the small, almost pointed chin, is more pronounced than ever. The thin lips tremble a little, not from age so much as from an excess of introspection. One would say that under that cover of extensive leafage, he had grown pallid and bloodless. The eyes wake up, and seem to peer out into space. Very gently, with a soft, toneless voice, he talks, at first uneasily, then fluently, with an exquisite simplicity, with no parade or self-assertion, without curiosity, of things at hand.

Benson, who had only seen him in company, expected once more to find him distrait and silent. On the contrary, he talked with instant effusion, mainly about Wessex, about places and houses, without the least affectation, of his own associations, and with reference to his own books. After lunch, we strolled into the garden, and a tree, over which it appeared I had once flung a shawl, was pointed out to us as now at least thirty feet in height. We were taken into the lawn and the croquet-ground, square places kept clear by a struggle with the superincumbent leafage, and looking like bright green rooms within dense walls of darker greenery. We wandered in close twilit corridors of foliage, once paths in the open garden, now almost subterranean passages in a sort of mysterious rabbit-warren. Here Hardy's life is spent, concealed from the world at large, shrinking (one would say) from the

105

light in the damp green shimmer of a dream, remote from experience, brooding on the past, consumed with a vague and hopeless melancholy, but brave and unupbraiding, if only preserved from disturbance.

The texture of his own old novels occupies him still. He spoke to me of having just been re-reading *Desperate Remedies*; he spoke as if it were some book written a long time ago, by someone who was no longer of much importance. "A melodrama, of course," he said; "but better as a story than one would think. Have you read it lately? Don't you think, just as a story it is rather good? Of course, I put all that in just in obedience to George Meredith. He said there must be a story. I did not care. The first book of all had no story at all. There was just the Woman interest. It is amusing to me that I thought I knew so much about women. I was so confident about it, knew exactly what they felt and what they wanted. That was what struck Meredith, the Woman interest in the book. But he said it would never do, so I tore it all up. The other day I found I had kept three or four pages of it; I think they must have been the worst, they were dreadfully bad. But about Women; I wonder how I came to write like that. Now I know them better, I should write just the same. I think I must be right – the women always hate it so. But I have said it all best in the poems, I suppose. I don't know; it is all so far away."

And *he* seemed so far away. We stayed two hours and a half. He was much brightened up by our visit, one could see that. His eyes were now wide open, a little red on his cheeks, the skin less puckered and parchment-like, as he waved farewell to us from the doorstep. He had been, for him, quite affectionate to me when we two were sitting alone in the garden; he talked then of our protracted friendship, of little incidents of more than thirty years ago. But one needs to have known him long to perceive that he is moved at all. He is so hushed, so irresponsive, so gently immobile. Old age has not, however, made him feeble; he seemed brisk and well, without any species of malady or incommodity. But it has accentuated his inwardness, his incapacity for any expression that is not quite superficial and unexcited. He remains, what he has always been, a sphinx-like little man, unrelated, unrevealed, displaying nothing that the most affectionate solicitude can make use of to explain the mystery of his magnificent genius.

A VACANT THRONE

On a solemn occasion in 1784 Gerard Hamilton wrote: "Samuel Johnson is dead. Let us go to the next best: there is nobody!" We should do a grave injustice to several younger veterans of genius if we declared that nobody can take the place of Thomas Hardy, since one or other of them will presently slip into pre-eminence. But, for the moment, there is no visible head to the profession of Letters in this country. The throne is vacant, and Literature is gravely bereaved.

It would be conventional, it would even be insincere, to allege that Literature has "lost" anything by Hardy's death. He preserved to a very great, perhaps to an unprecedented, age the power of expression, and it will be found that even in his 88th year he added something to his life's achievement. But practically his work was over; the cup was drained to its final drop, although the wine was excellent to the last. It is not in actual production that we have anything to regret; the loss is in the presence of the man himself, in his dignified and beautiful position as the unquestioned representative of living English Literature. Till last Wednesday, if an Englishman of culture was asked, "Who is the present head of your Literature?" instinctively, without fear of discussion, he answered: "Why, of course, Thomas Hardy!"

*

It is of great benefit to the intellectual life of a country that the years of a very great writer should be prolonged. It brings all other manifestations of talent into focus; it gives them proportion. In the case of Hardy, everything contrived to give dignity to his situation. His modesty, his serenity, his equipoise of taste, combined with the really extraordinary persistence of his sympathy and curiosity, made him an object of affectionate respect to old and young alike. He had outlived all adverse comment; he seemed to have entered into immortality without ceasing to be the simplest of mortals. It has been my privilege to enjoy his friendship for fifty-three years – a long span – and all through that time I have watched with care the development of his fame, which was at one time grossly and fanatically attacked. Looking back over that long period, I am struck by the concinnity of his intellectual career. In his calmness, in his retirement, in his rigorous probity, he was always unconsciously preparing for revered length of days and for an unchallenged predominance.

This is not the moment for making a pronouncement about the

character of Hardy's works in detail. They will occupy a hundred pens, and will be subjected to close analysis by every variety of commentator. It is the fashion to over-estimate his poetry, which will require to be sifted and selected. It is the fashion to underrate his novels, which form a solid contribution to the monument of English Literature. Criticism will hold the balance more evenly, and will show that this remarkable man was equally distinguished in the two arts of prose and verse. He kept the two completely distinct, yet always closely related.

*

In both there is dominant the note of what he very much disliked to hear called "pessimism", but what may be more accurately defined in words of his own as "the sad science of renunciation". He needed all the natural magic of his genius to prevent his work, interpenetrated as it was by this resigned and hopeless melancholy, from becoming sterile, but joy streamed into it from other sources – the joy of observation, of sympathy, of humour. Yet, after all, the core of Hardy's genius was austere and tragical, and this has to be taken into consideration, and weighed in every estimate of his writings. It was a curious fact, and difficult to explain, that this obvious aspect of his temperament was the one which he firmly refused to contemplate. The author of *Tess of the d'Urbervilles* conceived himself to be an optimist.

*

The external life of Thomas Hardy was uneventful to the last degree. He took a quiet part in the local business of the province which he made so illustrious. He travelled little; he made few and unobtrusive public appearances; he neither shrank from company nor courted it. Those who saw him superficially thought him unexhilarating; to appreciate his wit and wisdom it was desirable to be alone with him. The close of his life was extremely serene, and I think perfectly happy. He was the object of devoted care and the closest sympathetic attention. Of this I must beware of saying too much:

> If this be she who, gentlest of the wise,
>   Taught, soothed, loved, honoured, the departed One,
> Let me not vex with inharmonious sighs
> The silence of that heart's accepted sacrifice.

1928.

Lady Dorothy Nevill

1827–1913

This portrait is one of three Gosse published in 1919 in his book *Some Diversions of a Man of Letters* under the title "Three Experiments in Portraiture". The other two were of Lord Cromer and Lord Redesdale. The portrait of Lady Dorothy Nevill is the only one that takes the form of an open letter and indeed I think it was the only time, in a lifetime crammed with different kinds of writing, that Gosse tried this experiment. The letter first appeared early in 1914, privately printed at the Chiswick Press in an edition of 32 copies, dated 1913.

* * *

AN OPEN LETTER

DEAR LADY BURGHCLERE,

When we met for the first time after the death of our friend, you desired me to produce what you were kind enough to call "one of my portraits." But the art of the portrait-writer is capricious, and at that time I felt wholly disinclined for the adventure. I excused myself on the ground that the three thick volumes of her reminiscences made a further portrait needless, and I reflected, though I did not say, that the difficulties of presenting the evanescent charm and petulant wit of Lady Dorothy were insuperable. I partly think so still, but your command has lingered in my memory all these months, and I have determined to attempt to obey you, although what I send you can be no "portrait," but a few leaves torn out of a painter-writer's sketch-book.

The existence of the three published volumes does, after all, not preclude a more intimate study, because they are confessedly exterior. They represent what she saw and heard, not what others perceived in her. In the first place, they are very much better written than she would have written them herself. I must dwell presently on the curious fact that, with all her wit, she possessed no power of sustained literary expression. Her Memoirs were composed, as you know, by Mr Ralph Nevill, who is a practised writer and not otherwise could they have been given to the public. On this point her own evidence is explicit. She wrote to me, in all the excitement of the success of the volume of 1906: "The Press has been wonderfully good to my little efforts, but to Ralph the better part is due, as, out of the tangled remnants of my brain, he extracted these old anecdotes of my early years." This is as bravely characteristic of her modesty as it is of her candour, but I think it shows that there is still room for some record of the more intimate features of her charming and elusive character. I take up my pencil, but with little hope of success, since no more formidable task could be set me. I will at least try to be, as she would have scorned me for not being, sincere.

My friendship with Lady Dorothy Nevill occupied more than a quarter of a century. I met her first in the house of Sir Redvers and Lady Audrey Buller in the winter of 1887, soon after their return from Ireland. She had done me the great honour of desiring that I should be invited to meet her. She had known my venerable relative, the zoologist, Thomas Bell of Selborne, and she had corresponded in years long past, about entomology, with my father. We talked together on that first occasion for hours, and it seems to me that I was lifted, without preliminaries, into her intimacy. From that afternoon, until I drank tea with her for the last time, ten days before her death, the precious link was never loosened.

In 1887, her great social popularity had not begun. She was, I now know, already near sixty, but it never occurred to me to consider her age. She possessed a curious static quality, a perennial youthfulness. Every one must have observed how like Watts' picture of her at twenty she still was at eighty-six. This was not preserved by any arts or fictile graces. She rather affected, prematurely, the dress and appearance of an elderly woman. I remember her as always the same, very small and neat, very pretty with her chiselled nose, the fair oval of her features, the slightly ironic, slightly meditative smile, the fascinating colour of the steady eyes, beautifully set in the head, with the eyebrows rather lifted as in a perpetual amusement of curiosity. Her head, slightly sunken

110

into the shoulders, was often poised a little sideways, like a bird's that contemplates a hemp-seed. She had no quick movements, no gestures; she held herself very still. It always appeared to me that, in face of her indomitable energy and love of observation, this was an unconscious economy of force. It gave her a very peculiar aspect; I remember once frivolously saying to her that she looked as though she were going to "pounce" at me; but she never pounced. When she had to move, she rose energetically and moved with determination, but she never wasted a movement. Her physical strength – and she such a tiny creature – seemed to be wonderful. She was seldom unwell, although, like most very healthy people, she bewailed herself with exaggerated lamentations whenever anything was the matter with her. But even on these occasions she defied what she called "coddling." Once I found her suffering from a cold, on a very chilly day, without a fire, and I expostulated. She replied, with a sort of incongruity very characteristic of her, "Oh! none of your hot bottles for me!" In her last hours of consciousness she battled with the doctor's insistence that she must have a fire in her bedroom, and her children had to conceal the flame behind screens because she threatened to get out of bed and put it out. Her marvellous physical force has to be insisted on, for it was the very basis of her character.

Her humorous petulance, her little sharp changes of voice, the malice of her downcast eyes, the calmness of her demure and easy smile – how is any impression to be given of things so fugitive? Her life, which had not been without its troubles and anxieties, became one of prolonged and intense enjoyment. I think that this was the main reason of the delight which her company gave to almost every one. She was like a household blaze upon a rainy day, one stretched out one's hands to be warmed. She guarded herself against the charge of being amiable. "It would be horrid to be amiable," she used to say, and, indeed, there was always a touch of sharpness about her. She was amused once because I told her she was like an acidulated drop, half sweet and half sour. "Oh! any stupid woman can be sweet," she said, "it's often another name for imbecile."

She had curious little prejudices and antipathies. I never fathomed the reason of her fantastic horror of the feasts of the Church, particularly of Christmas. She always became curiously agitated as the month of December waned. In her notes she inveighed, in quaint alarm, against the impending "Christmas pains and penalties." I think she disliked the disturbance of social arrangements

111

which these festivals entailed. But there was more than that. She was certainly a little superstitious, in a mocking, eighteenth-century sort of way, as Madame du Deffand might have been. She constantly said, and still more frequently wrote, "D.V." after any project, even of the most frivolous kind. The idea was that one should be polite all round, in case of any contingency. When she was in the Riviera, she was much interested to hear that the Prince of Monaco had built and endowed a handsome church at Monte Carlo. "Very clever of him," she said, "for you never can tell."

Lady Dorothy's entire absence of affectation was eminently attractive. She would be mistress of herself, though China fell. Her strange little activities, her needlework, her paperwork, her collections, were the wonder of everybody, but she did not require approval; she adopted them, in the light of day, for her own amusement. She never pushed her peculiarities on the notice of visitors, but, at the same time, if discovered in the act of some incredible industry, she went on with it calmly. When she was in Heidelberg in 1892 and successive years, what interested her was the oddity of the students' life; she expatiated to me on their beer and their sabre-cuts. Whenever I went abroad of late years, I was exhorted to send her picture post-cards from out-of-the-way places, and "Remember that I like vulgar ones best," she added imperturbably. The story is perhaps known to you of how, in a circle of superfine ladies, the conversation turned to food, and the company outdid one another in protestations of delicacy. This one could only touch a little fruit, and that one was practically confined to a cup of tea. Lady Dorothy, who had remained silent and detached, was appealed to as to her opinion. In a sort of loud cackling – a voice she sometimes surprisingly adopted – she replied, "Oh, give me a blow-out of tripe and onions!" to the confusion of the *précieuses*. She had a wholesome respect for food, quite orthodox and old-fashioned, although I think she ate rather markedly little. But she liked that little good. She wrote to me once from Cannes, "This is not an intellectual place, but then the body rejoices in the cooking, and thanks God for that." She liked to experiment in foods, and her guests sometimes underwent strange surprises. One day she persuaded old Lord Wharncliffe, who was a great friend of hers, to send her a basket of guinea-pig, and she entertained a very distinguished company on a fricassee of this unusual game. She refused to say what the dish was until every one had heartily partaken, and then Mr George Russell turned suddenly pale and fled from the room. "Nothing but fancy,' remarked the hostess, composedly. When several years ago there was a proposal that we should feed upon horse-flesh, and a purveyor of that dainty opened a shop in Mayfair, Lady Dorothy was one of the first of his customers. She sallied forth in person, followed by a footman with a basket, and bought a joint in the presence of a jeering populace.

She had complete courage and absolute tolerance. Sometimes she pretended to be timid or fanatical, but that was only her fun. Her toleration and courage would have given her a foremost place among philanthropists or social reformers, if her tendencies had been humanitarian. She might have been another Elizabeth Fry, another Florence Nightingale. But she had no impulse whatever towards active benevolence, nor any interest in masses of men and women. And, above all, she was not an actor, but a spectator in life, and she evaded, often with droll agility, all the efforts which people made to drag her into propagandas of various kinds. She listened to what they had to say, and she begged for the particulars of specially awful examples of the abuses they set out to remedy. She was all sympathy and interest, and the propagandist started with this glittering ally in tow; but he turned, and where was she? She had slipped off, and was in contemplation of some other scheme of experience.

She described her life to me, in 1901, as a "treadmill of friendship, perpetually on the go"; and later she wrote: "I am hampered by perpetual outbursts of hospitality in every shape." Life was a spectacle to her, and society a congeries of little *guignols*, at all of which she would fain be seated, in a front stall. If she complained that hospitality "hampered" her, it was not that it interfered with any occupation or duty, but simply that she could not eat luncheon at three different houses at once. I remember being greatly amused when I congratulated her on having enjoyed some eminent public funeral, by her replying, grudgingly: "Yes – but I lost another most interesting ceremony through its being at the same hour." She grumbled: "People are tugging me to go and see things," not from any shyness of the hermit or reluctance to leave her home, but simply because she would gladly have yielded to them all. "Such a nuisance one can't be in two places at once, like a bird!" she remarked to me.

In this relation, her attitude to country life was droll. After long indulgence in her amazing social energy in London, she would suddenly become tired. The phenomenon never ceased to surprise her; she could not recollect that she had been tired before, and this must be the end of all things. She would fly to the country;

113

to Dorsetshire, to Norfolk, to Haslemere, to what she called "the soberness of Ascot." Then would come letters describing the bliss of rural calm. "Here I am! Just in time to save my life. For the future, no clothes and early hours." That lasted a very short while. Then a letter signed "Your recluse, D.N.," would show the dawn of a return to nature. Then *boutades* of increasing vehemence would mark the rising impatience. Sept. 12: "How dreadful it is that the country is so full of ladies." Sept. 15: "I am surrounded by tall women and short women, all very tiresome." Sept. 20: "So dull here, except for one pleasant episode of a drunken house-maid." Sept. 23: "Oh! I am so longing for the flesh-pots of dear dirty old London"; and then one knew that her return to Charles Street would not be long delayed. She was very fond indeed of country life, for a short time, and she was interested in gardens, but she really preferred streets. "Eridge is such a paradise – especially the quadrupeds," she once wrote to me from a house in which she found peculiar happiness. But she liked bipeds best.

However one may postpone the question, sooner or later it is necessary to consider the quality of Lady Dorothy Nevill's wit, since all things converge in her to that. But her wit is so difficult to define that it is not surprising that one avoids, as long as possible, coming actually to grips with it. We may lay the foundation of a formula, perhaps, by saying that it was a compound of solid good sense and an almost reckless whimsicality of speech. The curious thing about it was that it was not markedly intellectual, and still less literary. It had not the finish of such wit as is preserved in anthologies of humour. Every one who enjoyed the conversation of Lady Dorothy must have perceived with annoyance how little he could take away with him. Her phrases did not often recur to please that inward ear, "which is the bliss of solitude." What she said seemed at the time to be eminently right and sane; it was exhilarating to a high degree; it was lighted up by merriment, and piquancy, and salt; but it was the result of a kind of magic which needed the wand of the magician; it could not be reproduced by an imitator. It is very unfortunate, but the fact has to be faced. When we tell our grandchildren that Lady Dorothy Nevill was the finest female wit of her age, they will ask us for examples of her talent, and we shall have very few to give.

She liked to discuss people better than books or politics or principles, although she never shrank from these. But it was what she said about human beings that kept her interlocutors hanging on her lips. She made extraordinarily searching strictures on persons, without malice, but without nonsense of any kind. Her own favourites were treated with reserve in this respect: it was as though they were put in a pen by themselves, not to be criticised so long as they remained in favour; and she was not capricious, was, on the contrary, conspicuously loyal. But they always had the impression that it was only by special licence that they escaped the criticism that every one else was subjected to. Lady Dorothy Nevill was a stringent observer, and no respecter of persons. She carried a bow, and shot at folly as it flew. But I particularly wish to insist on the fact that her arrows, though they were feathered, were not poisoned.

Light was thrown on the nature of Lady Dorothy's wit by her correspondence. She could in no accepted sense be called a good letter-writer, although every now and then brilliantly amusing phrases occurred in her letters. I doubt whether she ever wrote one complete epistle; her correspondence consisted of tumultuous, reckless, sometimes extremely confused and incorrect notes, which, however, repeated – for those who knew how to interpret her language – the characteristics of her talk. She took no pains with her letters, and was under no illusion about their epistolary value. In fact, she was far too conscious of their lack of form, and would sign them, "Your incompetent old friend"; there was generally some apology for "this ill-written nonsense," or "what stuff this is, not worth your reading!" She once wrote to me: "I should like to tell you all about it, but alas! old Horace Walpole's talent has not descended on me." Unfortunately, that was true; so far as literary expression and the construction of sentences went, it had not. Her correspondence could never be given to the world, because it would need to be so much revised and expanded and smoothed out that it would no longer be hers at all.

Nevertheless, her reckless notes were always delightful to receive, because they gave the person to whom they were addressed a reflection of the writer's mood at the moment. They were ardent and personal, in their torrent of broken sentences, initials, mis-spelt names and nouns that had dropped their verbs. They were not so good as her talk, but they were like enough to it to be highly stimulating and entertaining; and in the course of them phrases would be struck out, like sparks from flint, which were nearly as good, and of the very same quality, as the things she used to say. She wrote her letters on a fantastic variety of strangely coloured paper, pink and blue and snuff-brown, violet and green and grey, paper that was stamped with patterns like a napkin, or frilled like a lace handkerchief, or embossed with for-get-me-nots like a child's valentine. She had tricks of time-saving;

always put "1" for "one,' and "x" for "cross," a word which she, who was never cross, loved to use. "I did not care for any of the guests; we seemed to live in a storm of x questions and crooked answers," she would write, or "I am afraid my last letter was rather x."

Lady Dorothy, as a letter-writer, had no superstitious reverence for the parts of speech . . . The spelling in her tumultuous notes threw a light upon that of very fine ladies in the seventeenth century. She made no effort to be exact, and much of her corre-spondence was made obscure by initials, which she expected her friends to interpret by divination. From a withering denunciation of the Government she expressly excepts Mr John Burns and "that much-abused Mr Birhell, whom I like." From about 1899 to 1903, I think that Lord Wolseley was the friend who occupied most of her thoughts. In her letters of those years the references to him are incessant, but when he is not "the F.M." and "our C.C.," she rings the changes on all possible forms of his name, from "Wollesley" to "Walsey" . . . She would laugh herself at her spell-ing, and would rebut any one who teased her about it by saying, "Oh! What does it matter? I don't pretend to be a bright specimen – like you!" When she made arrangements to come to see me at the House of Lords, which she frequently did, she always wrote it "the Lord's House," as though it were a conventicle.

One curious observation which the recipient of hundreds of her notes is bound to make, is the remarkable contrast between the general tone of them and the real disposition of their writer. Lady Dorothy Nevill in person was placid, indulgent, and calm; she never raised her voice, or challenged an opinion, or asserted her individuality. She played, very consistently, her part of the amused and attentive spectator in the theatre of life. But in her letters she pretended to be, or supposed herself called upon to seem, passionate and distracted. They are all twinkling with humorous or petulant exaggeration. She happens to forget an engagement, which was of no sort of importance, and this is how she apologises –

"To think that every hour since you said you would come I have repeated to myself – Gosse at 5, Gosse at 5, and then after all to go meandering off and leaving you to cuss and swear on the doorstep, and you will never come again now, really. No punishment here or hereafter will be too much for me. Lead me to the Red Hill Asylum, and leave me there."

This was written nearly twenty years ago, and she was not less vivacious until the end. Lord Lansdowne tells me of an anonymous

116

letter which he once received, to which she afterwards pleaded guilty. A cow used to be kept at the back of Lansdowne House, and the animal, no doubt feeling lonely, was in the habit of lowing at all sorts of hours. The letter, which was supposed to voice the complaint of the neighbours in Charles Street, was couched in the broadest Wiltshire dialect, and ended with the postscript: "Dang 'un, there'ee goes again!" As a matter of fact, her letters, about which she had no species of vanity or self-consciousness, were to her merely instruments of friendship. There was an odd mingling of affection and stiffness in them. She marshalled her acquaintances with them, and almost invariably they were concerned with arrangements for meeting or explanations of absence. In my own experience, I must add that she made an exception when her friends were abroad, when she took considerable pains to tell them the gossip, often in surprising terms. I was once regaled with her experiences as the neighbour of a famous African magnate, and with the remark, "Mrs ———," a London fine lady of repute, "has been here, and has scraped the whole inside out of Mr ———, and gone her way rejoicing." Nor did she spare the correspondent himself: – "Old Dr ——— has been here, and tells me he admires you very much; but I believe he has lost his memory, and he never had good taste at any time."

This was not a tribute which self-esteem could hug to its bosom. Of a very notorious individual she wrote to me: –

"I thought I should never be introduced to him, and I had to wait 100 years, but everything is possible in the best of worlds, and he was very satisfactory at last." Satisfactory! No word could be more characteristic on the pen of Lady Dorothy. To be "satisfactory," whether you were the President of the French Republic or Lord Wolseley or the Human Elephant (a pathetic freak in whom she took a great interest), was to perform on the stage of life, in her unruffled presence, the part which you had been called upon by Providence to fill. Even a criminal might be "satisfactory" if he did his job thoroughly. The only entirely unsatisfactory people were those who were insipid, conventional, and empty. "The first principle of society should be to extinguish the bores," she once said. I remember going with her to the Zoo in 1898, and being struck with a remark which she made, not because it was important, but because it was characteristic. We were looking at the wolves, which she liked; and then, close by, she noticed some kind of Indian cow. "What a bore for the wolves to have to live opposite a cow!" and then, as if talking to herself, "I do hate a ruminant!"

Her relations to literature, art, and science were spectacular also. She was a sympathetic and friendly onlooker, always on the side of those things against the Philistines, but not affecting special knowledge herself. She was something of a virtuoso. She once said, "I have a passion for reading, but on subjects which nobody else will touch," and this indicated the independence of her mind. She read to please herself, and to satisfy her thirst for experience. When our friendship began, Zola was in the act of producing the tremendous series of his Rougon–Macquart novels. It was one of our early themes of conversation. Zola was then an object of shuddering horror to the ordinary English reader. Lady Dorothy had already read *L'Assommoir*, and had not shrunk from it; so I ventured to tell her of *La Terre*, which was just appearing. She wrote to me about it: "I have been reading Zola. He takes the varnish off rural life, I must say. Oh! these horrid demons of Frenchmen know how to write. Even the most disgusting things they know how to describe poetically. I wish Zola could describe Haslemere with all the shops shut, rain falling, and most of the inhabitants in their cups." She told me later – for we followed our Zola to *Lourdes* and *Paris* – that some young Oxford prig saw *La Bête Humaine* lying on the table at Charles Street, and remarked that Lady Dorothy could surely not be aware that that was "no book for a lady." She said, "I told him it was just the book for me!"

She read Disraeli's novels over again, from time to time, with a renewal of sentiment. "I am dedicating my leisure hours to *Endymion*. What a charm after the beef and mutton of ordinary novels!" She gradually developed a cult for Swinburne, whom she had once scorned; in her repentance after his death, she wrote: "I never hear enough about that genius Swinburne! My heart warms when I think of him and read his poems." I think she was very much annoyed that he had never been a visitor at Charles Street. When Verlaine was in England, to deliver a lecture, in 1894, Lady Dorothy was insistent that, as I was seeing him frequently, I should bring the author of *Parallelement* to visit her. She said – I think under some illusion – "Verlaine is one of my pet poets, though," she added, "not of this world." I was obliged to tell her that neither Verlaine's clothes, nor his person, nor his habits, admittted of his being presented in Mayfair, and that, indeed, it was difficult to find a little French eating-house in Soho where he could be at home. She then said: "Why can't you take me to see him in this eating-house?" I had to explain that of the alternatives that was really the least possible. She was not pleased.

Nor am I pleased with this attempt of mine to draw the features of our wonderful fairy friend. However I may sharpen the pencil, the line it makes is still too heavy. I feel that these anecdotes seem to belie her exquisite refinement, the rapidity and delicacy of her mental movement. To tell them is like stroking the wings of a moth. Above all, it is a matter of despair to attempt to define her emotional nature. Lady Dorothy Nevill was possessed neither of gravity nor of pathos; she was totally devoid of sentimentality. This made it easy for a superficial observer to refuse to believe that the author of so many pungent observations and such apparently volatile cynicism had a heart. When this was once questioned in company, one who knew her well replied: "Ah! yes, she has a heart, and it is like a grain of mustard-seed!" But her kindliness was shown, with great fidelity, to those whom she really honoured with her favour. I do not know whether it would be strictly correct to say that she had the genius of friendship, because that supposes a certain initiative and action which were foreign to Lady Dorothy's habits. But she possessed, to a high degree, the genius of comradeship. She held the reins very tightly, and she let no one escape whom she wished to retain. She took immense pains to preserve her friendships, and indeed became, dear creature, a little bit tyrannical at last. Her notes grew to be excessively emphatic. She would begin a letter quite cheerfully with "Oh, you demon!" or complain of "total and terrible neglect of an old friend; I could fill this sheet of paper with an account of your misdeeds!" She was ingenious in reproach: "I cannot afford to waste penny after penny, and no assets forthcoming," or "I have only two correspondents, and one of them is a traitor; I therefore cease to write to you for ever!" This might sound formidable, but it was only one of the constant surprises of her humour, and would be followed next day by the most placable of notelets.

Her curiosity with regard to life spread to her benevolences, which often took somewhat the form of voyages of discovery. Among these her weekly excursion to the London Hospital, in all weathers and in every kind of cheap conveyance, was prominent. I have to confess that I preferred that a visit to her should not be immediately prefaced by one of these adventures among the "pore dear things" at the hospital, because that was sure to mean the recital of some gruesome operation she had heard of, or the details of some almost equally gruesome cure. She enjoyed the whole experience in a way which is blank to the professional humanitarian, but I suspect the "pore dear things" appreciated her listening smile and sympathetic worldliness much more than

119

they would have done the admonitions of a more conscious philanthropist.

And, indeed, in retrospect, it is her kindliness that shines forth. She followed all that her friends did, everything that happened to those who were close to them. She liked always to receive the tribute of what she called my "literary efforts," and was ruthlessly sharp in observing announcements of them: "Publishing again, and of course no copy for poor old me," when not a volume had yet left the binders. She took up absurd little phrases with delightful *camaraderie*; I have forgotten why at one time she took to signing herself "Your Koh-i-Noor," and wrote: "If I can hope to be the Koh-i-Noor of Mrs Gosse's party, I shall be sure to come on Monday." One might go on indefinitely reviving these memories of her random humour and kindly whimsicality. But I close on a word of tenderer gravity, which I am sure will affect you. She had been a little tyrannical, as usual, and perhaps thought the tone of her persiflage rather excessive; a few hours later came a second note, which began: "You have made my life happier for me these last years – you, and Lady Airlie, and dearest Winifred." From her who never gave way to sentimentality in any form, and who prided herself on being as rigid as a nut-cracker, this was worth all the protestations of some more ebullient being. And there, dear Lady Burghclere, I must leave this poor sketch for such approval as you can bring yourself to give it.

Very faithfully yours,
EDMUND GOSSE.

January 1914.

Henry James
1843–1916

Gosse's long essay on James first appeared in *The London Mercury* in April and May, 1920 and was reprinted in *Aspects and Impressions* in 1922. It begins with a consideration of the light James himself threw on his own early literary adventures in the prefaces to the New York edition of his novels. Gosse confessed himself, though "constitutionally fitted to take pleasure in the accent of almost everything that Henry James ever wrote", rather disappointed. James had told Gosse he intended to abandon "all restraints of conventional reticence" in relating the circumstances in which each story was written, but somehow he had not done so. Fortunately James had then embarked on his autobiography, but he had only taken the tale up to a time before Gosse met him when he died leaving *The Middle Years* unfinished, to be edited by Percy Lubbock after his death.

The part of Gosse's essay printed here takes up the story just before the time of Gosse's own personal knowledge. The nature of the friendship between James and Gosse had been described by Leon Edel as "literary-gossipy". (In 1885, soon after his return from America, Gosse wrote to William Dean Howells "Last week I dined with Henry James at the Reform Club, to satisfy his craving for gossip, which proved insatiable".) But the essay, though it shows a degree of reticent formality itself, indicates too, as Gosse puts it, "a flash or glimpse of deeper things" in their relationship.

* * *

After [a] fruitful year in Paris, the first result of which was the publication in London of his earliest surviving novel, *Roderick Hudson*, and the completion of *The American*, Henry James left his "glittering, charming, civilized Paris" and settled in London.

121

He submitted himself, as he wrote to his brother William in 1878, "without reserve to that Londonizing process of which the effect is to convince you that, having lived here, you may, if need be, abjure civilization and bury yourself in the country, but may not, in pursuit of civilization, live in any smaller town." He plunged deeply into the study of London, externally and socially, and into the production of literature, in which he was now as steadily active as he was elegantly proficient. These novels of his earliest period have neither the profundity nor the originality of those of his middle and final periods, but they have an exquisite freshness of their own, and a workmanship the lucidity and logic of which he owed in no small measure to his conversations with Daudet and Maupassant, and to his, at that time almost exclusive, reading of the finest French fiction. He published *The American* in 1877, *The Europeans* and *Daisy Miller* in 1878, and *An International Episode* in 1879. He might advance in stature and breadth; he might come to disdain the exiguous beauty of these comparatively juvenile books, but now at all events were clearly revealed all the qualities which were to develop later, and to make Henry James unique among writers of Anglo-Saxon race.

His welcome into English society was remarkable if we reflect that he seemed to have little to give in return for what it offered except his social adaptability, his pleasant and still formal amenity, and his admirable capacity for listening. It cannot be repeated too clearly that the Henry James of those early days had very little of the impressiveness of his later manner. He went everywhere sedately, watchfully, graciously, but never prominently. In the winter of 1878–79 it is recorded that he dined out in London 107 times, but it is highly questionable whether this amazing assiduity at the best dinner-tables will be found to have impressed itself on any Greville or Crabb Robinson who was taking notes at the time. He was strenuously living up to his standard, "my charming little standard of wit, of grace, of good manners, of vivacity, of urbanity, of intelligence, of what makes an easy and natural style of intercourse." He was watching the rather gross and unironic, but honest and vigorous, English upper middle-class of that day with mingled feelings, in which curiosity and a sort of remote sympathy took a main part. At 107 London dinners he observed the ever-shifting pieces of the general kaleidoscope with tremendous acuteness, and although he thought their reds and yellows would have been improved by a slight infusion of the Florentine harmony, on the whole he was never weary of watching their evolutions. In this way the years slipped by, while he made a thousand acquaintances and a dozen durable friendships. It is a matter of pride and happiness to me that I am able to touch on one of the latter.

It is often curiously difficult for intimate friends, who have the impression in later years that they must always have known one another, to recall the occasion and the place where they first met. That was the case with Henry James and me. Several times we languidly tried to recover those particulars, but without success. I think, however, that it was at some dinner-party that we first met, and as the incident is dubiously connected with the publication of the *Hawthorne* in 1879, and with Mr (now Lord) Morley, whom we both frequently saw at that epoch, I am pretty sure that the event took place early in 1880. The acquaintance, however, did not "ripen," as people say, until the summer of 1882, when in connexion with an article on the drawings of George Du Maurier, which I was anxious Henry James should write – having heard him express himself with high enthusiasm regarding these works of art – he invited me to go to see him and to talk over the project. I found him, one sunshiny afternoon, in his lodgings on the first floor of No. 3 Bolton Street, at the Piccadilly end of the street, where the houses look askew into Green Park. Here he had been living ever since he came over from France in 1876, and the situation was eminently characteristic of the impassioned student of London life and haunter of London society which he had now become.

Stretched on the sofa and apologizing for not rising to greet me, his appearance gave me a little shock, for I had not thought of him as an invalid. He hurriedly and rather evasively declared that he was not that, but that a muscular weakness of his spine obliged him, as he said, "to assume the horizontal posture" during some hours of every day in order to bear the almost unbroken routine of evening engagements. I think that this weakness gradually passed away, but certainly for many years it handicapped his activity. I recall his appearance, seen then for the first time by daylight; there was something shadowy about it, the face framed in dark brown hair cut short in the Paris fashion, and in equally dark beard, rather loose and "fluffy." He was in deep mourning, his mother having died five or six months earlier, and he himself having but recently returned from a melancholy visit to America, where he had unwillingly left his father, who seemed far from well. His manner was grave, extremely courteous, but a little formal and frightened, which seemed strange in a man living in constant communication with the world. Our business regarding

Du Maurier was soon concluded, and James talked with increasing ease, but always with a punctilious hesitancy, about Paris, where he seemed, to my dazzlement, to know even a larger number of persons of distinction than he did in London.

He promised, before I left, to return my visit, but news of the alarming illness of his father called him suddenly to America. He wrote to me from Boston in April, 1883, but he did not return to London until the autumn of that year. Our intercourse was then resumed, and, immediately, on the familiar footing which it preserved, without an hour's abatement, until the sad moment of his fatal illness. When he returned to Bolton Street – this was in August, 1883 – he had broken all the ties which held him to residence in America, a country which, as it turned out, he was not destined to revisit for more than twenty years. By this means Henry James became a homeless man in a peculiar sense, for he continued to be looked upon as a foreigner in London, while he seemed to have lost citizenship in the United States. It was a little later than this that that somewhat acidulated patriot Colonel Higginson, in reply to someone who said that Henry James was a cosmopolitan, remarked, "Hardly! for a cosmopolitan is at home even in his own country!" This condition made James, although superficially gregarious, essentially isolated, and though his books were numerous and were greatly admired, they were tacitly ignored alike in summaries of English and of American current literature. There was no escape from this dilemma. Henry James was equally determined not to lay down his American birthright and not to reside in America. Every year of his exile, therefore, emphasized the fact of his separation from all other Anglo-Saxons, and he endured, in the world of letters, the singular fate of being a man without a country.

The collection of his private letters, therefore, which has now been published under the sympathetic editorship of Mr Percy Lubbock, reveals the adventures of an author who, long excluded from two literatures, is now eagerly claimed by both of them, and it displays those movements of a character of great energy and singular originality which circumstances have hitherto concealed from curiosity. There was very little on the surface of his existence to bear evidence to the passionate intensity of the stream beneath. This those who have had the privilege of seeing his letters know is marvellously revealed in his private correspondence. A certain change in his life was brought about by the arrival in 1885 of his sister Alice, who, in now confirmed ill-health, was persuaded to make Bournemouth and afterwards Leamington her home. He could not share her life, but at all events he could assiduously diversify it by his visits, and Bournemouth had a second attraction for him in the presence of Robert Louis Stevenson, with whom he had by this time formed one of the closest of his friendships. Stevenson's side of the correspondence has long been known, and it is one of the main attractions which Mr Lubbock held out to his readers that Henry James's letters to Stevenson are now published. No episode of the literary history of the time is more fascinating than the interchange of feeling between these two great artists. The death of Stevenson, nine years later than their first meeting, though long anticipated, fell upon Henry James with a shock which he found at first scarcely endurable. For a long time afterwards he could not bring himself to mention the name of R L S without a distressing agitation.

In 1886 the publication of *The Bostonians*, a novel which showed an advance in direct or, as it was then styled, "realistic" painting of modern society, increased the cleft which now divided him from his native country, for *The Bostonians* was angrily regarded as satirizing not merely certain types, but certain recognizable figures in Massachusetts, and that with a suggestive daring which was unusual. Henry James, intent upon making a vivid picture, and already perhaps a little out of touch with American sentiment, was indignant at the reception of this book, which he ultimately, to my great disappointment, omitted from his Collected Edition, for reasons which he gave in a long letter to myself. Hence, as his works now appear, *The Princess Casamassima*, of 1886, an essentially London adventure story, takes its place as the earliest of the novels of his second period, although preceded by admirable short tales in that manner, the most characteristic of which is doubtless *The Author of Beltraffio* (1885). This exemplifies the custom he had now adopted of seizing an incident reported to him, often a very slight and bald affair, and weaving round it a thick and glittering web of silken fancy, just as the worm winds round the unsightly chrysalis its graceful robe of gold. I speak of *The Author of Beltraffio*, and after thirty-five years I may confess that this extraordinarily vivid story was woven around a dark incident in the private life of an eminent author known to us both, which I, having told Henry James in a moment of levity, was presently horrified and even sensibly alarmed to see thus pinnacled in the broad light of day.

After exhausting at last the not very shining amenities of his lodgings in Bolton Street, where all was old and dingy, he went westward in 1886 into Kensington, and settled in a flat which was both new and bright, at 34 De Vere Gardens, Kensington, where he began a novel called *The Tragic Muse*, on which he expended an immense amount of pains. He was greatly wearied by the effort, and not entirely satisfied with the result. He determined, as he said, "to do nothing but short lengths" for the future, and he devoted himself to the execution of *contes*. But even the art of the short story presently yielded to a new and, it must be confessed, a deleterious fascination, that of the stage. He was disappointed – he made no secret to his friends of his disillusion – in the commercial success of his novels, which was inadequate to his needs. I believe that he greatly over-estimated these needs, and that at no time he was really pressed by the want of money. But he thought that he was, and in his anxiety he turned to the theatre as a market in which to earn a fortune. Little has hitherto been revealed with regard to this "sawdust and orange-peel phase" (as he called it) in Henry James's career, but it cannot be ignored any longer. The memories of his intimate friends are stored with its incidents, his letters will be found to be full of it.

Henry James wrote, between 1889 and 1894, seven or eight plays, on each of which he expended an infinitude of pains and mental distress. At the end of this period, unwillingly persuaded at last that all his agony was in vain, and that he could never secure fame and fortune, or even a patient hearing from the theatre-going public by his dramatic work, he abandoned the hopeless struggle. He was by temperament little fitted to endure the disappointments and delays which must always attend the course of a dramatist who has not conquered a position which enables him to browbeat the tyrants behind the stage. Henry James was punctilious, ceremonious, and precise; it is not to be denied that he was apt to be hasty in taking offence, and not very ready to overlook an impertinence. The whole existence of the actor is lax and casual; the manager is the capricious leader of an irresponsible band of egotists. Henry James lost no occasion of dwelling, in private conversation, on this aspect of an amiable and entertaining profession. He was not prepared to accept young actresses at their own valuation, and the happy-go-lucky democracy of the "mimes" as he bracketed both sexes, irritated him to the verge of frenzy.

It was, however, with a determination to curb his impatience, and with a conviction that he could submit his idiosyncracies to what he called the "passionate economy" of play-writing, that he began, in 1889, to dedicate himself to the drama, excluding for the time being all other considerations. He went over to Paris in the winter of that year, largely to talk over the stage with

Alphonse Daudet and Edmond de Goncourt, and he returned to put the finishing touches on *The American*, a dramatic version of one of his earliest novels. He finished this play at the Palazzo Barbaro, the beautiful home of his friends, the Daniel Curtises, in Venice, in June, 1890, thereupon taking a long holiday, one of the latest of his extended Italian tours, through Venetia and Tuscany. Edward Compton had by this time accepted *The American*, being attracted by his own chances in the part of Christopher Newman. When Henry James reappeared in London, and particularly when the rehearsals began, we all noticed how deeply the theatrical virus had penetrated his nature. His excitement swelled until the evening of January 3, 1891, when *The American* was acted at Southport by Compton's company in anticipation of its appearance in London. Henry James was kind enough to wish me to go down on this occasion with him to Southport, but it was not possible. On the afternoon of the ordeal he wrote to me from the local hotel: "After eleven o'clock to-night I *may* be the world's – you know – and I may be the undertaker's. I count upon you and your wife both to spend this evening in fasting, silence, and supplication. I will send you a word in the morning, a wire if I can." He was "so nervous that I miswrite and misspell."

The result, in the provinces, of this first experiment was not decisive. It is true that he told Robert Louis Stevenson that he was enjoying a success which made him blush. But the final result in London, where *The American* was not played until September, 1891, was only partly encouraging. Henry James was now cast down as unreasonably as he had been uplifted. He told me that "the strain, the anxiety, the peculiar form and colour of the ordeal (not to be divined in the least in advance)" had "sickened him to *death*." He used language of the most picturesque extravagance about the "purgatory" of the performances, which ran at the Opera Comique for two months. There was nothing in the mediocre fortunes of this play to decide the questions whether Henry James was or was not justified in abandoning all other forms of art for the drama. We endeavoured to persuade him that, on the whole, he was not justified, but he swept our arguments aside, and he devoted himself wholly to the infatuation of his sterile task.

The American had been dramatized from a published novel. Henry James now thought that he should do better with original plots, and he wrote two comedies, the one named *Tenants* and the other *Disengaged*, of each of which he formed high expectations. But, although they were submitted to several managers, who gave them their customary loitering and fluctuating attention, they were in every case ultimately refused. Each refusal plunged the dramatist into the lowest pit of furious depression from which he presently emerged with freshly-kindled hopes. Like the moralist, he never was but always to be blest. *The Album* and *The Reprobate* – there is a melancholy satisfaction in giving life to the mere names of these stillborn children of his brain – started with wild hopes and suffered from the same complete failure to satisfy the caprice of the managers. At the close of 1893, after one of these "sordid developments," he made up his mind to abandon the struggle. But George Alexander promised that, if he would but persevere, he really and truly would produce him infallibly at no distant date, and poor Henry James could not but persevere. "I mean to wage this war ferociously for one year more," and he composed, with infinite agony and deliberation, the comedy of *Guy Domville*.

The night of January 5, 1895, was the most tragical in Henry James's career. His hopes and fears had been strung up to the most excruciating point, and I think that I have never witnessed such agonies of parturition. *Guy Domville* – which has never been printed – was a delicate and picturesque play, of which the only disadvantage that I could discover was that instead of having a last scene which tied up all the threads in a neat conclusion, it left all those threads loose as they would be in life. George Alexander was sanguine of success, and to do Henry James honour such a galaxy of artistic, literary, and scientific celebrity gathered in the stalls of the St. James's Theatre as perhaps were never seen in a London playhouse before or since. Henry James was positively storm-ridden with emotion before the fatal night, and full of fantastic plans. I recall that one was that he should hide in the bar of a little public-house down an alley close to the theatre, whither I should slip forth at the end of the second act and report "how it was going." This was not carried out, and fortunately Henry James resisted the temptation of being present in the theatre during the performance. All seemed to be going fairly well until the close, when Henry James appeared and was called before the curtain – only to be subjected – to our unspeakable horror and shame – to a storm of hoots and jeers and catcalls from the gallery, answered by loud and sustained applause from the stalls, the whole producing an effect of hell broke loose, in the midst of which the author, as white as chalk, bowed and spread forth deprecating hands and finally vanished. It was said at the time, and confirmed later, that this horrible performance was not intended to humiliate

128

Henry James, but was the result of a cabal against George Alexander.

Early next morning I called at 34 De Vere Gardens, hardly daring to press the bell for fear of the worst of news, so shattered with excitement had the playwright been on the previous evening. I was astonished to find him perfectly calm; he had slept well and was breakfasting with appetite. The theatrical bubble in which he had lived a tormented existence for five years was wholly and finally broken, and he returned, even in that earliest conversation, to the discussion of the work which he had so long and so sadly neglected, the art of direct prose narrative. And now a remarkable thing happened. The discipline of toiling for the caprices of the theatre had amounted, for so redundant an imaginative writer, to the putting on of a mental strait-jacket. He saw now that he need stoop no longer to what he called "a meek and lowly review of the right ways to keep on the right side of a body of people who have paid money to be amused at a particular hour and place." Henry James was not released from this system of vigorous renunciation without a very singular result. To write for the theatre, the qualities of brevity and directness, of an elaborate plainness, had been perceived by him to be absolutely necessary and he had tried to cultivate them with dogged patience for five years. But when he broke with the theatre, the rebound was excessive. I recall his saying to me, after the fiasco of *Guy Domville*, "At all events, I have escaped for ever from the foul fiend Excision!" He vibrated with the sense of release, and he began to enjoy, physically and intellectually, a freedom which had hitherto been foreign to his nature.

*

The abrupt change in Henry James's outlook on life, which was the result of his violent disillusion with regard to theatrical hopes and ambitions, took the form of a distaste for London and a determination, vague enough at first, to breathe for the future in a home of his own by the sea. He thought of Bournemouth, more definitely of Torquay, but finally his fate was sealed by his being offered, for the early summer months of 1896, a small house on the cliff at Point Hill, Playden, whence he could look down, as from an "eagle's nest," on the exquisite little red-roofed town of Rye and over the wide floor of the marsh of Sussex. When the time came for his being turned out of this retreat he positively

129

could not face the problem of returning to the breathless heat of London in August, and he secured the Vicarage in the heart of Rye itself for two months more. Here, as earlier at Point Hill, I was his guest, and it was wonderful to observe how his whole moral and intellectual nature seemed to burgeon and expand in the new and delicious liberty of country life. We were incessantly in the open air, on the terrace (for the Vicarage, though musty and dim, possessed, like the fresher Point Hill, a sea-looking terrace), sauntering round the little town, or roving for miles and miles over the illimitable flats, to Winchelsea, to Lydd, to the recesses of Walland Marsh – even, on one peerless occasion, so far afield as to Midley Chapel and the Romneys.

Never had I known Henry James so radiant, so cheerful or so self-assured. During the earlier London years there had hung over him a sort of canopy, a mixture of reserve and deprecation, faintly darkening the fullness of communion with his character; there always had seemed to be something indefinably non-conductive between him and those in whom he had most confidence. While the play-writing fit was on him this had deepened almost into fretfulness; the complete freedom of intercourse which is the charm of friendship had been made more and more difficult by an excess of sensibility. Henry James had become almost what the French call a *buisson d'épines*. It was therefore surprising and highly delightful to find that this cloud had ceased to brood over him, and had floated away, leaving behind it a laughing azure in which quite a new and charming Henry James stood revealed. The summer of 1896, when by a succession of happy chances I was much alone with him at Rye, rests in my recollection as made exquisite by his serene and even playful uniformity of temper, by the removal of everything which had made intercourse occasionally difficult and by the addition of forms of amenity that had scarcely been foreshadowed. On reflection, however, I find that I am mixing up memories of June at Point Hill and of September at the Vicarage with the final Rye adventure, which must now be chronicled. When he was obliged to turn out of his second refuge, he returned to London, but with an ever-deepening nostalgia for the little Sussex town where he had been happy. In the following summer the voice of Venice called him so loudly that he stayed in London longer than usual, meaning to spend the autumn and winter in Italy. He thought meanwhile of Bournemouth and of Saxmundham. He went on his bicycle round the desolate ghost of Dunwich, but his heart was whispering "Rye" to him all the while. Nothing then seemed available, however, when suddenly the unexpected vacancy of the most eligible residence conceivable settled, in the course of a couple of days, the whole future earthly pilgrimage of Henry James. The huge fact was immediately announced in a letter of September 25, 1897:

> I am just drawing a long breath from having signed – a few moments since – a most portentous parchment: the lease of a smallish, charming, cheap old house in the country – down at Rye – for 21 years. (It was built about 1705.) It is exactly what I want and secretly and hopelessly coveted (since knowing it) without dreaming it would ever fall. But it *has* fallen – and has a beautiful room for you (the King's Room – George II's – who slept there); together with every promise of yielding me an indispensable retreat from May to October (every year). I hope you are not more sorry to take up the load of life that awaits, these days, the hunch of one's shoulders than I am. You'll ask me what I mean by "life." Come down to Lamb House and I'll tell you.

There were the most delightful possibilities in the property, which included a small garden and lawn, the whole hemmed in by a peaceful old red wall, plentifully tapestried with espaliers. The noble tower of Rye church looked down into it, and Henry James felt that the chimes sounded sweetly to him as he faced his garden in monastic quiet, the little market-town packed tightly about him, yet wholly out of sight.

Meanwhile the intellectual release had been none the less marked than the physical. The earliest result of his final escape from the lures of the Vivian of the stage had been the composition of a novel, *The Spoils of Poynton*, in a manner entirely different from that of his earlier long romances. This was published in 1897, and in the meantime he had set to work on a longer and more ambitious romance, *What Maisie Knew*. In these he began the exercise of what has been called his "later manner," which it would be out of proportion to attempt to define in a study which purports to be biographical rather than critical. It is enough to remind the reader familiar with Henry James's writings that in abandoning the more popular and conventional method of composition he aimed at nothing less than a revolution in the art of the novelist . . .

The first novel actually completed at Lamb House was *The Awkward Age*, which was ready for the printers early in 1898. The ecstasy with which he settled down to appreciate his new surroundings is reflected in that novel, where the abode of Mr Longdon is neither more nor less than a picture of Lamb House.

It was a wonderful summer and autumn, and, as Henry James said: "The air of the place thrilled all the while with the bliss of birds, the hum of little lives unseen, and the flicker of white butterflies." The MS of *The Awkward Age* was no sooner finished than he took up the germ of an incident dimly related to him years before at Addington, by Archbishop Benson, and wove it into *The Turn of the Screw*, a sort of moral (or immoral) ghost story which not a few readers consider to be the most powerful of all his writings, and which others again peculiarly detest. I admit myself to be a hanger-on of the former group, and I have very vivid recollections of the period when *The Turn of the Screw* was being composed. The author discussed it with a freedom not usual with him. I remember that when he had finished it he said to me one day: "I had to correct the proofs of my ghost story last night, and when I had finished them I was so frightened that I was afraid to go upstairs to bed!"

By the close of 1898 he had got rid of the flat in De Vere Gardens, which had become a mere burden to him, and had taken what he called an "invaluable south-looking Carlton-Gardens-sweeping bedroom" at the Reform Club in Pall Mall, which served his brief and sudden pilgrimages to town for many seasons. Lamb House, in the course of this year, became his almost exclusive residence, and it is to be noted that at the same time a remarkable change came over the nature of his correspondence. He had been a meticulous but not very inspired letter-writer in early youth; his capacity for epistolary composition and his appetite for it had developed remarkably in the middle years (1882–1890). During the hectic period of his theatrical ambition it had dwindled again. But when he settled finally at Rye, spreading himself in luxurious contentment within the protection of his old brick garden-wall, the pink and purple surface of which stood in his fancy as a sort of bodyguard of security passed down for that particular purpose through mild ages of restfulness as soon as he sat, with his household gods about him, in the almost cotton-woolly hush of Lamb House, he began to blossom out into a correspondent of a new and splendid class. The finest and most characteristic letters of Henry James start with his fifty-fifth year, and they continue to expand in volume, in richness and in self-revelation almost to the close of his life. On this subject Mr Percy Lubbock, than whom no one has known better the idiosyncrasies of Henry James, has described his method of correspondence in a passage which could not be bettered:

The rich apologies for silence and backwardness that preface so many of his letters must be interpreted in the light, partly indeed of his natural luxuriance of phraseology, but much more of his generous conception of the humblest correspondent's claim on him for response. He could not answer a brief note of friendliness but with pages of abounding eloquence. He never dealt in the mere small change of intercourse; the post-card and the half-sheet did not exist for him; a few lines of enquiry would bring from him a bulging packet of manuscript overwhelming in its disproportion. No wonder that with this standard of the meaning of a letter he often groaned under his postal burden. He discharged himself of it, in general, very late at night; the morning's work left him too much exhausted for more composition until then. At midnight he would sit down to his letter-writing and cover sheet after sheet, sometimes for hours, with his dashing and not very readable script. Occasionally he would give up a day to the working off of arrears by dictation, seldom omitting to excuse himself to each correspondent in turn for the infliction of the "fierce legibility" of type.

This amplitude of correspondence was the outcome of an affectionate solicitude for his friends, which led him in another direction, namely, in that of exercising a hospitality towards them for which he had never found an opportunity before. He did not, however, choose to collect anything which might remotely be called "a party"; what he really preferred was the presence of a single friend at a time, of a companion who would look after himself in the morning, and be prepared for a stroll with his host in the afternoon, and for a banquet of untrammelled conversation under the lamp or on the expanse of the lawn after the comfortable descent of nightfall.

His practice in regard to such a visitor was always to descend to the railway station below the town to welcome the guest, who would instantly recognize his remarkable figure hurrying along the platform. Under the large soft hat would be visible the large pale face, anxiously scanning the carriage-windows and breaking into smiles of sun-shine when the new-comer was discovered. Welcome was signified by both hands waved aloft, lifting the skirts of the customary cloak, like wings. Then, luggage attended to, and the arm of the guest securely seized, as though even now there might be an attempt at escape, a slow ascent on foot would begin up the steep streets, the last and steepest of all leading to a discreet door which admitted directly to the broad hall of Lamb House. Within were, to right and left, the pleasant old rooms, with low windows opening straight into the garden, which was so sheltered and economized as to seem actually spacious. Further to the left was a lofty detached room, full of books and lights, where in summer Henry James usually wrote, secluded from all possible disturbance. The ascent of arrival from the railway grew to be more and more interesting as time went on, and as the novelist became more and more a familiar and respected citizen, it was much interrupted at last by bows from ladies and salaams from shop-keepers; many little boys and girls, the latter having often curtsied, had to be greeted and sometimes patted on the head. These social movements used to inspire in me the inquiry: "Well, how soon are you to be the Mayor-Elect of Rye?" a pleasantry which was always well received. So obviously did Henry James, in the process of years, become the leading inhabitant that it grew to seem no impossibility. Stranger things had happened! No civic authority would have been more conscientious and few less efficient.

His outward appearance developed in accordance with his moral and intellectual expansion. I have said that in early life Henry James was not "impressive"; as time went on his appearance became, on the contrary, excessively noticeable and arresting. He removed the beard which had long disguised his face, and so revealed the strong lines of mouth and chin, which responded to the majesty of the skull. In the breadth and smoothness of the head – Henry James became almost wholly bald early in life – there was at length something sacerdotal. As time went on, he grew less and less Anglo-Saxon in appearance and more Latin. I remember once seeing a Canon preaching in the Cathedral of Toulouse who was the picture of Henry James in his unction, his gravity, and his vehemence. Sometimes there could be noted – what Henry would have hated to think existing – a theatrical look which struck the eye, as though he might be some retired *jeune premier* of the Français, *jeune* no longer; and often the prelatical expression faded into a fleeting likeness to one or other celebrated Frenchman of letters (never to any Englishman or American), somewhat of Lacordaire in the intolerable scrutiny of the eyes, somewhat of Sainte-Beuve, too, in all except the mouth, which, though mobile and elastic, gave the impression in rest of being small. All these comparisons and suggestions, however, must be taken as the barest hints, intended to mark the tendency of Henry James's radically powerful and unique outer appearance. The beautiful modelling of the brows, waxing and waning under the stress of excitement, is a point which singularly dwells in the memory.

It is very difficult to give an impression of his manner, which was complex in the extreme, now restrained with a deep reserve, now suddenly expanding, so as to leave the auditor breathless, into a flood of exuberance. He had the habit of keeping his friends apart from one another; his intimacies were contained in many watertight compartments. He disliked to think that he was the subject of an interchange of impressions, and though he who discussed everybody and everything with the most penetrating and analyzing curiosity must have known perfectly well that he also, in his turn, was the theme of endless discussion, he liked to ignore it and to feign to be a bodiless spectator. Accordingly, he was not apt to pay for the revelations, confidences, guesses and what not which he so eagerly demanded and enjoyed by any coin of a similar species. He begged the human race to plunge into experiences, but he proposed to take no plunge himself, or at least to have no audience when he plunged.

So discreet was he, and so like a fountain sealed, that many of those who were well acquainted with him have supposed that he was mainly a creature of observation and fancy, and that life stirred his intellect while leaving his senses untouched. But every now and then he disclosed to a friend, or rather admitted such a friend to a flash or glimpse of deeper things. The glimpse was never prolonged or illuminated, it was like peering down for a moment through some chasm in the rocks dimmed by the vapour of a clash of waves. One such flash will always leave my memory dazzled. I was staying alone with Henry James at Rye one summer, and as twilight deepened we walked together in the garden. I forget by what meanders we approached the subject, but I suddenly found that in profuse and enigmatic language he was recounting to me an experience, something that had happened, not something repeated or imagined. He spoke of standing on the pavement of a city, in the dusk, and of gazing upwards across the misty street, watching, watching for the lighting of a lamp in a window on the third storey. And the lamp blazed out, and through bursting tears he strained to see what was behind it, the unapproachable face. And for hours he stood there, wet with the rain, brushed by the phantom hurrying figures of the scene and never from behind the lamp was for one moment visible the face. The mysterious and poignant revelation closed, and one could make no comment, ask no questions, being throttled oneself by an overpowering emotion. And for a long time Henry James

135

shuffled beside me in the darkness, shaking the dew off the laurels, and still there was no sound at all in the garden but what our heels made crunching the gravel, nor was the silence broken when suddenly we entered the house and he disappeared for an hour . . .

*

In the summer of 1902 Mrs Wharton, who had dedicated to him, as a stranger, her novel of *The Valley of Decision*, became a personal acquaintance, and soon, and till the end, one of the most valued and intimate of his friends. This event synchronized with the publication of his own great book, *The Wings of a Dove*. It was followed by *The Golden Bowl*. He now turned from such huge schemes as this – which in his fatigue he described as "too inordinately drawn out and too inordinately rubbed in" – to the composition of short stories, in which he found both rest and refreshment.

On this subject, the capabilities of the *conte* as a form of peculiarly polished and finished literature, he regaled me – and doubtless other friends – at this time with priceless observations. I recall a radiant August afternoon when we sallied from his high abode and descended to the mud of the winding waters of the Brede, where, on the shaky bridge across the river, leaning perilously above the flood, Henry James held forth on the extraordinary skill of Guy de Maupassant, whose posthumous collection, *Le Colporteur*, had just reached him, and on the importance of securing, as that inimitable artist so constantly secured, one straight, intelligible action which must be the source of all vitality in what, without it, became a mere wandering anecdote, more or less vaguely ornamented . . .

In 1904 . . . just before his plan for visiting the United States had taken shape, he had promised to write for a leading firm of English publishers "a romantical-psychological-pictorial-social" book about London, and in November, 1905, he returned to this project with vivacity. There is a peculiar interest about works that great writers mean to compose and never succeed in producing, and this scheme of a great picturesque book about London is like a ghost among the realities of Henry James's invention. He spoke about it more often and more freely than he did about his solid creations; I feel as though I had handled and almost as though I had read it. Westminster was to have been the core of the matter, which was to circle out concentrically to the City and the suburbs.

Henry James put me under gratified contribution by coming frequently to the House of Lords in quest of "local colour," and I took him through the corridors and up into garrets of the Palace where never foreign foot had stepped before. There was not, to make a clean breast of it, much "local colour" to be wrung out, but Henry James was indefatigable in curiosity. What really did thrill him was to stand looking down from one of the windows of the Library on the Terrace, crowded with its motley afternoon crew of Members of both Houses and their guests of both sexes. He liked that better than to mingle with the throng itself, and he should have written a superb page on the scene, with its background of shining river and misty towers. Alas! it will not be read until we know what songs the Sirens sang.

All through the quiet autumn and winter of 1906 he was busy preparing the collective and definite, but far from complete, edition of his novels and tales which began to appear some twelve months later. This involved a labour which some of his friends ventured to disapprove of, since it included a re-writing into his latest style of the early stories which possessed a charm in their unaffected immaturity. Henry James was conscious, I think of the arguments which might be brought against this reckless revision, but he rejected them with violence. I was spending a day or two with him at Lamb House when *Roderick Hudson* was undergoing, or rather had just undergone, the terrible trial; so the revised copy, darkened and swelled with MS. alterations, was put into my hands. I thought – I dare say I was quite mistaken – that the whole perspective of Henry James's work, the evidence of his development and evolution, his historical growth, were confused and belied by this wholesale tampering with the original text. Accordingly I exclaimed against such dribbling of new wine into the old bottles. This was after dinner, as we sat alone in the garden-room. All that Henry James – though I confess, with a darkened countenance – said at the time was, "The only alternative would have been to put the vile thing" – that is to say the graceful tale of *Roderick Hudson* – "behind the fire and have done with it!" Then we passed to other subjects, and at length we parted for the night in unruffled cheerfulness. But what was my dismay, on reaching the breakfast-table next morning, to see my host sombre and taciturn, with gloom thrown across his frowning features like a veil. I inquired rather anxiously whether he had slept well. "Slept!" he answered with dreary emphasis. "Was I likely to sleep when my brain was tortured with all the cruel and – to put it plainly to you – monstrous insinuations which you had brought forward against my proper, my necessary, my absolutely inevitable corrections of the disgraceful and disreputable style of *Roderick Hudson*?" I withered, like a guilty thing ashamed, before the eyes that glared at me over the coffee-pot, and I inly resolved that not one word of question should ever escape my lips on this subject again . . .

The "nightmare," as he called it, of his Collected Edition kept him closely engaged – it ultimately ran into a range of twenty-four volumes – but . . . he seemed to be approaching old age in placidity and satisfaction when, towards the end of 1909, he was seized by a mysterious group of illnesses which "deprived him of all power to work and caused him immeasurable suffering of mind." Unfortunately his beloved brother William was also failing in health, and had come to Europe in the vain search for recovery; their conditions painfully interacted. The whole year 1910 was one of almost unmitigated distress. Henry accompanied Mr and Mrs William back to their home in New Hampshire, where in the autumn not only the eminent philosopher, but a third brother, Robertson James, died, leaving Henry solitary indeed, and weighed upon by a cloud of melancholy which forbade him to write or almost to speak. Out of this he passed in the spring of 1911, and returned to Lamb House where he had another sharp attack of illness in the autumn of 1912. It was now felt that the long pale winters over the marsh at Rye were impossible for him, and the bedroom at the Reform Club insufficient. He therefore rented a small flat high up over the Thames in Cheyne Walk, where he was henceforth to spend half of each year and die. He sat, on the occasion of his seventieth birthday, to Mr Sargent for the picture which is now one of the treasures of the National Portrait Gallery; this was surprisingly mutilated, while being exhibited at the Royal Academy, by a "militant suffragette"; Henry James was extraordinarily exhilarated by having been thus "impaired by the tomahawk of the savage," and displayed himself as "breasting a wondrous high-tide of postal condolence in this doubly-damaged state." This was his latest excitement before the war with Germany drowned every other consideration.

The record of the last months of Henry James's life is told in the wonderful letters that he wrote between the beginning of August 1914, and the close of November, 1915. He was at Rye when the war broke out, but he found it absolutely impossible to stay there without daily communication with friends in person, and, contrary to his lifelong habit, he came posting up to London in the midst of the burning August weather. He was transfigured by the events of those early weeks, overpowered, and yet, in his vast and generous excitement, himself overpowering. He threw off all the languor and melancholy of the recent years, and he appeared actually grown in size as he stalked the streets, amazingly moved by the unexpected nightmare, "the huge horror of blackness" which he saw before him. "The plunge of civilization into the abyss of blood and darkness by the wanton feat of these two infamous autocrats" made him suddenly realize that the quiet years of prosperity which had preceded 1914 had been really, as he put it, "treacherous," and that their perfidy had left us unprotected against the tragic terrors which now faced our world. It was astonishing how great Henry James suddenly seemed to become; he positively loomed above us in his splendid and disinterested faith. His first instinct had been horror at the prospect; his second anger and indignation against the criminals; but to these succeeded a passion of love and sympathy for England and France, and an unyielding but anxious and straining confidence in their ultimate success . . . To be in his company was to be encouraged, stimulated and yet filled with a sense of the almost intolerable gravity of the situation; it was to be moved with that "trumpet note" in his voice, as the men fighting in the dark defiles of Roncevaux were moved by the sound of the oliphant of Roland. He drew a long breath of relief in the thought that England had not failed in her manifest duty to France nor "shirked any one of the implications of the Entente." When, as at the end of the first month, things were far from exhilarating for the Allies, Henry James did not give way to despair, but he went back to Rye, possessing his soul in waiting patience, "bracing himself unutterably," as he put it, "and holding on somehow (though to God knows what!) in presence of the perpetrations so gratuitously and infamously hideous as the destruction of Louvain and its accompaniments."

At Lamb House he sat through that gorgeous tawny September, listening to the German guns thundering just across the Channel, while the advance of the enemy through those beautiful lands which he knew and loved so well filled him with anguish. He used to sally forth and stand on the bastions of his little town, gazing over the dim marsh that became sand-dunes, and then sea, and then a mirage of the white cliffs of French Flanders that were actually visible when the atmosphere grew transparent. The anguish of his execration became almost the howl of some animal, of a lion of the forest with the arrow in his flank, when the Germans wrecked Reims Cathedral. He gazed and gazed over the sea southeast, and fancied that he saw the flicker of the flames. He ate and drank, he talked and walked and thought, he slept and waked and lived and breathed only the War. His friends grew anxious, the tension was beyond what his natural powers, transfigured as they were, could be expected to endure, and he was persuaded to come back to Chelsea, although a semblance of summer still made Rye attractive.

During this time his attitude towards America was marked by a peculiar delicacy. His letters expressed no upbraiding, but a yearning, restrained impatience that took the form of a constant celebration of the attitude of England, which he found in those early months consistently admirable . . . For his own part, almost immediately on his return to London in October, 1914, Henry James began to relieve the mental high pressure by some kinds of practical work for which nothing in his previous life had fitted him, but into which he now threw himself with even exhausting ardour. He had always shrunk from physical contact with miscellaneous strangers, but now nothing seemed unwelcome save aloofness which would have divided him from the sufferings of others. The sad fate of Belgium particularly moved him, and he found close to his flat in Cheyne Walk a centre for the relief of Belgian refugees, and he was active in service there. A little later on he ardently espoused the work of the American Volunteer Motor Ambulance Corps. His practical experiences and his anxiety to take part in the great English movement for the relief of the Belgians and the French are reflected in the essays which were collected in 1919 under the title of *Within the Rim*.

We were, however, made anxious by the effect of all this upon his nerves. The magnificent exaltation of spirit which made him a trumpeter in the sacred progress of the Allies was of a nature to alarm us as much as it inspirited and rejoiced us. When we thought of what he had been in 1911, how sadly he had aged in 1912, it was not credible that in 1915 he could endure to be filled to overflowing by this tide of febrile enthusiasm. Some of us, in the hope of diverting his thoughts a little from the obsession of the war, urged him to return to his proper work; and he responded in part to our observations, while not abandoning his charitable service. He was at work on *The Ivory Tower* when the war began, but he could not recover the note of placidity which it demanded, and he abandoned it in favour of a novel begun in 1900 and then laid aside, *The Sense of the Past*. He continued, at the same time, his reminiscences, and was writing the fragment published since his death as *The Middle Years*. But all this work was forced from him with an effort, very slowly; the old sprightly running of

140

composition was at an end, the fact being that his thoughts were now incessantly distracted by considerations of a far more serious order.

The hesitations of Mr Wilson, and Henry James's conviction that in the spring of 1915 the United States government was "sitting down in meekness and silence under the German repudiation of every engagement she solemnly took with" America, led to his taking a step which he felt to be in many respects painful, but absolutely inevitable. His heart was so passionately united with England in her colossal effort, and he was so dismally discouraged by the unending hesitation of America, that he determined to do what he had always strenuously refused to do before, namely, apply for British naturalization. Mr Asquith (then Prime Minister), Sir George Prothero (the Editor of the *Quarterly Review*), and I had the honour and the gratification of being chosen his sponsors. In the case of so illustrious a claimant the usual formalities were passed over, and on July 26th, 1915, Henry James became a British subject. Unhappily he did not live to see America join the Allies, and so missed the joy for which he longed above all others.

But his radiant enthusiasm was burning him out. In August he had a slight breakdown, and his autumn was made miserable by an affection of the heart. He felt, he said, twenty years older, but "still, I cultivate, I at least attempt, a brazen front." He still got about, and I saw him at Westminster on the evening of November 29th. This was, I believe, the last time he went out, and two days later, on the night between the 1st and the 2nd of December, he had a stroke. He partly rallied and was able to receive comfort from the presence of his sister-in-law, Mrs William James, who hurried across the Atlantic to nurse him. At the New Year he was awarded the highest honour which the King can confer on a British man of letters, the Order of Merit, the insignia of which were brought to his bedside by Lord Bryce. On February 28th, 1916, he died, within two months of his 73rd birthday. His body was cremated, and the funeral service held at that "altar of the dead" which he had loved so much, Chelsea Old Church, a few yards from his own door.

1920.

Notes

Abbreviations used in the Notes and the Index

ACS	Swinburne	HJ	James
AT	Tennyson	NPG	National Portrait Gallery
BM	British Museum	RB	Browning
CP	Patmore	RHH	Horne
CR	Christina Rossetti	RK	Kipling
DN	Dorothy Nevill	RLS	Stevenson
DNB	*Dictionary of National Biography*	*SOED*	*Shorter Oxford English Dictionary*
EG	Gosse	TH	Hardy
EG	*Edmund Gosse: a literary landscape* by Ann Thwaite (1984)	WB	Wolcott Balestier
		WW	Whitman
F&S	*Father and Son* by Edmund Gosse (1907)		

ROBERT LOUIS STEVENSON

p. 10   **"a former schoolfellow"**   Mansel Dames. See *EG* pp. 48, 64–5. He is the boy in *F&S* who has tastes "singularly parallel to my own".

"in the Hebrides"   For more on EG's Scottish tour, see *EG* pp. 90–1. EG also referred to this early meeting in an address to the First Annual Dinner of the RLS Club, 13 November 1920 in Edinburgh. It is printed in *I Can Remember RLS* ed. Rosaline Masson, 1922.

"Professor Blackie"   This is presumably John Stuart Blackie who had a summer home near Oban. (See *DNB*)

Sam Bough   (1822–1878) has a number of pictures in the National Gallery of Scotland. According to DNB, he was "a thorough Bohemian" with "a fine bass voice". Bough supplied many landscape illustrations for Blackie books. RLS wrote his obituary in the *Academy*, 30 November 1878.

142

p. 11 **"in the interests of a deer-forest"** The notorious clearing by heartless landlords was then at its height.

"some remote lighthouse" RLS's father, uncle and grandfather were lighthouse engineers.

Sidney Colvin (1845–1927), art and literary critic. At this time, Slade Professor of Fine Art at Cambridge and Director of the Fitzwilliam Museum.

p. 12 **"as Constance does of Arthur"** "There was not such a gracious creature born." Shakespeare *King John*, Act III Sc.IV.

p. 13 **Academe or Mouseion** EG is thinking of the sort of talk that presumably went on in Plato's Academy and in the "Museion" founded by one of the Ptolemies in Alexandria.

Leslie Stephen (1832–1904), most famous now as Virginia Woolf's father, was then editor of the *Cornhill*.

An Inland Voyage was a canoe tour in Belgium and France.

Mr Lang Andrew Lang (1844–1912), a prolific writer, who is now best known for his collections of fairy tales.

p. 14 **Queen-Mother and Rosamond** This was Swinburne's first proper book, two plays dated 1860.

p. 15 **The Amateur Emigrant from the Clyde to Sandy Hook** was published in Chicago in 1895.

Across the Plains, with other memories and essays was published in London and New York in 1892.

Berkeley Square EG referred to this evening in a letter to RLS in October, 1879 "Many times, in a blue spot, I have lived over again the dismal clammy evening when we bid one another farewell at the corner of Berkeley Square, and have betted sixpence with my soul I should never see your face again . . . I have found out your existence is very important to me."

p. 16 **Ouida** was the pen-name of a popular writer, Marie Louise de la Ramée (1839–1908). She published 45 novels and was then at the height of her fame.

"a charming lady" Fanny Osbourne (1840–1914) was a divorced American, ten years older than RLS. For EG's relationship with her, see *EG* p. 219.

Walter Pollock (1850–1926), at that time a sub-editor on the *Saturday Review*, which he edited from 1883–1894.

W E Henley (1849–1903), poet and editor, was one of RLS's closest friends.

p. 17 **John Addington Symonds** (1840–93), scholar of Italian, critic and poet, had also gone to Switzerland for his health, arriving there in August 1877.

"adventure in a thornwood" To Colvin, RLS wrote of "adventure in a thornbush".

"Hazlitt's character" Leslie Stephen (*DNB*) writes of his "excessive touchiness", CP of his "ingrained selfishness".

Liber Amoris was published in 1823. De Quincey called it an "explosion of frenzy" necessary to "empty the overburdened spirit". It was written in the aftermath of Hazlitt's love affair with Sarah Walker, who would not marry him after he had obtained a divorce from his first wife.

craniology phrenology, the study of skulls.

Austin Dobson (1840–1921), poet and biographer. For many years he was a colleague of EG at the Board of Trade.

Mr Saintsbury George Saintsbury (1845–1933), critic and French scholar. In 1895 he became professor of English Literature at Edinburgh.

Jean Cavalier (1681–1740), was a leading figure, not in Scottish history as EG seems to suggest, but in the 1702 revolt in the Cevennes. At the end of an extraordinary life, Cavalier became Lieutenant-Governor of Jersey.

p. 18   **"booming"**   Partridge's *Dictionary of Slang and Unconventional English* calls it the "effective launching of any goods". With regard to books, it is now usually called "hype".

John Morley's *English Men of Letters* series   (1878–1919) eventually contained 60 volumes, including one on RLS himself by Stephen Gwynn. Early contributors included a number now almost totally fogotten, such as William Black (on *Goldsmith*) and Principal Shairp (*Burns*), as well as Leslie Stephen's *Johnson*. EG himself contributed *Gray* in 1882 and Henry James *Hawthorne* in 1883.

Victoria   Her favourite residence, Balmoral, was not far off.

p. 19   **"long afterward . . . an account"**   "My First book: *Treasure Island*" *The Idler*, August 1894.

Mr Osbourne   Lloyd was then 13.

Davos Press   Facsimiles of the publications are reproduced in the Swanston edition of the Works of RLS, vol.22.

p. 20   **Story of the Red Barn**   The most famous telling of this story (*Maria Marten and the Red Barn*) was a staple of Victorian popular theatre. The real-life murder took place in 1827.

"dead leaves in Vallombrosa"   from Milton "Paradise Lost" 1.303.

"certain mountains as graceful . . . "   RLS to EG 20 May 1883.

"beg Gilder your prettiest"   RLS to EG dated by Colvin April 1883, not September.

Gilder   is Richard Watson Gilder (1844–1909), from 1881 until his death editor of the *Century* magazine, based in New York. EG was for some time London agent of the *Century*.

p. 21   **"Pulvis et Umbra"**   From Horace *Odes* IV.7 "[we are but] dust and shadow". RLS used the phrase as the title of an essay which appeared in *Scribner's* in April 1888 and in 1892 in *Across the Plains*.

Skerryvore   The house was RLS's father's gift to Fanny, named after the lighthouse which was "the most beautiful and the most difficult to build of all the lighthouses erected by his family", according to RLS's biographer, Graham Balfour.

"never able to go to Bournemouth"   There had been a slight misunderstanding in 1886. See *EG* p. 273.

Mr Colvin's house   Sidney Colvin (see above) was entitled to lodgings in the Museum after his appointment as Keeper of Prints and Drawings in 1883.

p. 22   **Mr Watts**   G F Watts (1817–1904) himself said "I paint ideas not things". The titles of his paintings included "Love and Death", "Hope", "Love Triumphant" etc.

"witnessing his will"   In fact, EG and "the housekeeper of the hotel" did witness the will.

p. 23   *Underwoods*   was published in August 1887. It was his first adult book of poems. In May, 1883 he wrote to Henley: "If I live till I am forty, I shall have a book of rhymes like Pollock, Gosse or whom you please. Really, I have begun to learn some of the rudiments of that trade."

The Woodlanders   was published on 15 March 1887. EG reviewed it in the 2 April *Saturday Review*, praising its "richness and humanity" but making some criticisms.

CHRISTINA ROSSETTI

p. 27 **"untimely death"** Dante Gabriel Rossetti died in 1882, aged only 54.

Gabriele Rossetti had been a librettist to the opera house in Naples and curator of antiquities at the museum there before fleeing to England via Malta, for political reasons. He became Professor of Italian at King's College, London in 1831.

p. 28 **G Polidori** CR was indeed the granddaughter of G Polidori but Gaetano Polidori (1764–1853) was a teacher of Italian in London. It was his son, Christina's uncle, J W Polidori (1795–1821), who was Byron's physician.

"a thorough Englishwoman" But CR was certainly bilingual and some of her poems were written in Italian.

p. 29 **"On Idlers and Idling"** RLS's "Apology for Idlers" appeared in the "Cornhill" in July 1877 and can be found in *Virginibus Puerisque* (1881).

Philistia the home of the Philistines, and so identified with people whose interests are "material and commonplace". (*SOED*)

"when she was eleven" G Polidori printed CR's birthday poem for her mother in 1842.

p. 30 **"Goblin Market"** was first published in 1862.

"chalk drawing in profile" This 1866 drawing is described as "a large crayon drawing" in H C Marillier: *Dante Gabriel Rossetti* (1899). It was exhibited in the great double exhibition of Rossetti's work in 1883, after his death. So also was the well-known image of the very young Christina in "The Girlhood of Mary Virgin" 1848–9.

"the high priestess of Pre-raphaelitism" Christina had been closely associated with the brotherhood as a contributor to *The Gem* and as sister of two of the main forces in the movement. One of their beliefs was in the beauty of the "natural" and there is nothing less natural than a crinoline.

"a pillar of cloud, a Sibyl" suggests someone awesome and of great wisdom. God appeared to Moses as a pillar of cloud (see Exodus 13:21 and 33:10). The Sibyls of ancient times foretold the future.

p. 31 **"the mysterious complaint"** In his *English Literature: An Illustrated Record* Vol.IV, EG says it was "a terrible and rare complaint, exophthalonic bronchocele".

Mr Theodore Watts later (1896) Watts-Dunton (1832–1914) contributed most frequently to the *Athenaeum*. Now he is mainly remembered for his guardianship of Swinburne at the Pines.

"Edith and Maggie . . . Flora". Gosse's slip was rather typical. Henry James once spoke of his "genius for inaccuracy".

Maria (1827–1876) became an Anglican nun towards the end of her life. She wrote "A Shadow of Dante: being an Essay towards studying himself, his World and his Pilgrimage" (1878).

p. 32 **Newton's influence on Cowper** John Newton (1725–1807) employed William Cowper (1731–1800) as a kind of lay-curate in his parish work in Olney in Buckinghamshire. Cowper composed hymns at Newton's request, including "God moves in a mysterious way". Leslie Stephen in the *DNB* says "Newton's kindness was unfailing, however injudicious may have been some of his modes of guidance." One commentator said, "The spirit of self-accusation pervades all Newton's writings."

"saw her for the last time" For EG's further contact with her, see *EG* p. 243 and note p. 536.

RICHARD HENGIST HORNE

p. 33   **"The publication of the love letters"**   was in 1899, in two volumes.
"the farthing epic"   See p. 37. Ann Blainey's biography of Horne (1968) is called *The Farthing Poet*.

p. 34   **"It was in 1874"**   Richard Garnett in DNB gives the date of the marriage as 1873.
Arthur O'Shaughnessy   (1844–1881) knew EG well as they worked together in the BM. See *EG* p. 72. His first book of poems was published in 1870 and attracted great admiration. His wife, Eleanor, died in 1879.
Westland Marston   (1819–1890) wrote plays in verse. His first, *The Patrician's Daughter* (1841), had a prologue by Dickens. He regarded *Strathmore*, a historical play, as his best work.
"still occasionally called"   is an interesting passing comment. The name is now, of course, totally established.
"all uninvited"   In a letter to a friend, Harry Edwards, in San Francisco, RHH described his own performance at the wedding thus: "A young gentleman by particular desire played a 'Bolero' on the guitar, with a song to match and was nearly overcome by three or four successive storms of applause."
"lately come back from Australia"   RHH had returned in September 1869.
Hazlitt   RHH's biographer tells the dramatic story of his going with Charles Wells to see the dying Hazlitt and finding him already in his coffin.

p. 35   **G H Lewes**   (1817–1878), the writer now chiefly remembered for his long relationship with George Eliot.
1802 or 1803   His birth certificate gave 31 December 1802.
his parents   James Horne, apparently a rather feckless soldier, died when the poet was a child. He was largely brought up by his grandmother and her second husband.
"quite solitary"   RHH was actually the eldest of three brothers. His brother James was important to him towards the end of his life.
"some foolish escapade"   According to his biographer (Blainey, *Farthing Poet*), RHH left Sandhurst after one year, having failed his examinations.
Charles Wells   (1799–1879) aroused Keats's wrath by a hoax on his friend, Keats's younger brother, Tom. *Joseph and his Brethren* was a play published under a pseudonym in 1823–4.

p. 36   **"should have entered Sandhurst"**   See above.
War of Mexican Independence   RHH was a midshipman aboard a Royal Naval ship loaned secretly to help Mexico in her fight for independence from Spain.
Baron Munchausen   (1720–1797) is proverbially associated with absurdly exaggerated tales of adventure. A collection ascribed to him was published in England in 1785.

p. 37   **Miss Mitford**   (1787–1855) was the author of *Our Village* and a close friend of Elizabeth Barrett Browning.
"little Miss Foggs"   RHH's bride was actually Catherine Clare St George Foggo. They were married on 17 June 1847, nine months after the Brownings.
"sought a southern hemisphere"   In April 1852 Australian gold arrived in England and inflamed the imaginations of many. RHH arrived in Melbourne in September 1852.
"oceans of correspondence"   The letters of Elizabeth Barrett Browning addressed to RHH were edited by S R T Mayer in two volumes in 1877 with a connecting narrative by RHH.

p. 38   **"republish his poems"**   The ninth and definitive edition of "Orion" was published in 1872 and *Cosmo de Medici* was reissued in 1875 with additional poems.

p. 39   *Prometheus, the Fire-Bringer*: **a drama in verse**   was published first in Edinburgh in 1864 and then in Melbourne in 1866.

     "his edition of her letters"   See above.

     "for economy's sake"   For many years, the postage on postcards was half that on letters.

p. 40   **your Terrace**   Hanover Terrace, Regent's Park, not far from Northumberland Street, now Luxborough Street, off the Marylebone Road.

p. 41   **Lisson Grove**   Paddington, now familiar to readers and playgoers as the home of Shaw's Eliza Dolittle.

ROBERT BROWNING

p. 44   **"cold gradations of decay"**   Dr Johnson in his poem "On the death of Mr R Levett."

     "in St Petersburg"   RB visited Russia in 1833 as a sort of private secretary to the Russian Consul-General in London, Chevalier George de Benckhausen.

     "in Warwick Crescent"   RB's house at 19 Warwick Crescent, where he lived from 1862 to 1887, was only a few minutes walk from EG's house at 29 Delamere Terrace where he lived from 1876 until after RB's death.

     "falls asleep in Italy"   RB died in Venice, in the Palazzo Rezzonico belonging to his son.

     "faint . . . yet pursuing"   as Gideon, Judges 8:4.

     "no better way than this"   One of RB's doctors to his son: "His death was what death ought to be, but rarely is."

p. 45   **"sofa-lap of leather"**   "ensconce in luxury's sofa-lap of leather!" from "Dubiety" in RB's last book *Asolando* (1889).

     Fellows' Garden of Trinity   The summer of 1889 was EG's last term as Clark Lecturer at Trinity.

p. 46   **"Paracelsus"**   published in 1835, won RB his first acclaim from the reviewers. John Forster named him "at once with Shelley, Coleridge and Wordsworth . . . he has in himself all the elements of a great poet."

     "Sordello"   published in 1840, but written over seven years, ran to almost 6 000 lines. Its obscurity caused damage to RB's reputation but it is now generally regarded as one of the finest long poems of the 19th century.

     "Bells and Pomegranates"   published in a series from 1841 to 1846. The first part was "Pippa Passes".

p. 47   **"as lately . . . he did err"**   EG may be referring to RB's habit of "unstoppable monologues" and his personal vanity in old age.

p. 48   **Colombe**   appeared in RB's play *Colombe's Birthday* which ran for just seven nights in 1853.

     "never doubted clouds would break"   from RB's "Asolando", 1889.

ALFRED TENNYSON

p. 50   **"salad days"**   Shakespeare: *Antony and Cleopatra* i,5,73.

"Maud"   (1855) had a special place in AT's heart; it always had both admirers and detractors.

"In Memoriam"   AT's poem in memory of his friend Arthur Hallam was published in 1850.

"forty years ago"   EG is speaking of a time long after their publication – of the 1870s.

"The Loves of the Wrens"   "The Window or The Song of the Wrens" had the subtitle "The Loves of the Wrens", first published with music by Arthur Sullivan in 1870.

"Enoch Arden"   published in 1864, when Matthew Arnold considered it "perhaps the best thing Tennyson has done".

"Lucretius"   published 1868, has been called by Christopher Ricks a "powerful dramatic monologue" "which compacts three of Tennyson's horrors: at erotic madness, at a Godless world, and at a juggernaut universe".

"the late Duke of Argyll"   8th Duke, George Douglas Campbell (1823–1900), known as the "Radical Duke", he held various posts in Whig administrations. R B Martin in his biography of AT calls the Duke 'one of his most constant, if not exactly intimate friends".

Gladstone   When Prime Minister, he was responsible for offering AT a baronetcy and later his peerage. He had not been entirely enthusiastic about earlier poems but "carried the 'Idylls' around in his pocket". 10,000 copies were sold within weeks of publication in June 1859.

"The Holy Grail"   published 1869. Christopher Ricks dates "Pelleas and Ettarre" as after "The Holy Grail", but there was then a considerable gap before "The Last Tournament" appeared in the *Contemporary Review* for December 1871.

summer of 1871   There is some doubt about the date. In a letter to W Bell Scott of 28 August 1874 EG wrote "Did I tell you I was presented by Ralston to Tennyson, who was very affable?" But EG did go to Norway in 1871 and AT went in 1858, which fits in with "some dozen years before" if it is 1871.

"transcribers on the BM staff"   EG had joined the BM staff in January 1867 at the age of 17.

p. 51   **Dotheboys Hall**   the execrable school in Dickens's *Nicholas Nickleby*.

W R S Ralston   (1828–1889) had joined the BM staff in 1853 and mastered Russian as he later encouraged EG to master the Scandinavian languages. He resigned through ill-health in 1875. He was a literary journalist and master storyteller.

God of the Golden Bow   Apollo, the god of poetry, was often depicted with a golden bow.

"or was I a worm . . . ?"   From "The Delphic Hymn to Apollo" by ACS.

James Spedding   (1808–1881), editor of Bacon's works. An "Apostle", he was at Cambridge with AT, who called him "the wisest man I know".

Mr Thornycroft's statue   The sculptor Hamo Thornycroft (1850–1925) was one of EG's closest friends. The seated figure was executed in marble in 1909.

Trinity College   AT's Cambridge college with which EG had a strong connection as Clark Lecturer.

p. 52   **Norway**   EG made two visits to Norway in 1871 and 1872. See *EG* pp. 106–7 and 126–8.

p. 52   **"my stammering verses"**   AT had presumably seen EG's first book *Madrigals, Songs and Sonnets* (with J A Blaikie, 1870).

  Antinous   born about AD 110 in Bithynia, his beauty and grace made him a favourite of Hadrian, who, after he was drowned in the Nile, insisted on his deification.

p. 53   **"as to appear censorious"**   EG's dissatisfaction with "the spectacle provided" was echoed by many who attended the funeral. Burne-Jones wrote "O but yesterday was so flat and flattening. I'll never forgive the Queen for not coming up to it . . . " R B Martin *Tennyson* p. 583.

  "a well-conducted . . . ceremony"   This is Walter Scott in his *Life of John Dryden* (1834), referring to his funeral on 13 May 1700.

p. 54   **"yet would we not disturb him . . . "**   EG adapted Matthew Arnold's poem "Westminster Abbey".

p. 55   **"quick succession" of deaths**   Matthew Arnold 15 April 1888, Robert Browning 12 December 1889, AT 6 October 1892.

  Victor Hugo   born 1802, had died in Paris in May 1885.

  Festus   P J Bailey's *Festus* was published in 1839.

  Rudyard Kipling   (1865–1936) was only 27 when EG was writing.

  William Watson   (1858–1935) had published *Wordsworth's Grave and other poems* in 1890; his *Lachrymae musarum* (1892) were verses on the death of Tennyson. EG raised a subscription for him the following year. See *EG* pp. 350–1.

  "only twice"   The first occasion is presumably that recorded in these pages, the second when EG visited Aldworth in August 1888 (see *EG* p. 296). The two occasions were 17 years apart (or 14 if EG had the BM date wrong). It was typical of EG to get the figure quite wrong: "about twelve years".

p. 56   **Swinburne on Tennyson**   He called "Idylls of the King" the "Morte d'Albert or Idylls of the Prince Consort" and thought very little of *Queen Mary* though, as he said, the *Spectator* set it "high above the ordinary work of Shakespeare . . . " It was performed in 1876.

  "And this I prophesy"   Dryden's "Epistle to Mr Congreve".

  roses without thorns   Compare *Paradise Lost* 1.256 "flowers of all time, and without thorn the rose".

  St Basil   Greek patriarch (329–379).

  "to this day"   It was only seven years since Hugo's death. See above. Two books were published posthumously.

p. 57   *Tit-Bits*   a popular weekly magazine founded in 1881 by George Newnes.

  Pearson's Weekly   was set up in 1890 to compete with *Tit-Bits*.

ALGERNON CHARLES SWINBURNE

p. 60   **Red Flag**   From its use in Roman times as a sign of war (displayed on the Capitol to assemble the Army for active service), the flag had become a signal of danger and defiance, and thus the banner of socialism and revolution.

  Victor Hugo   (1802–1885), French novelist, poet and dramatist, best known now for *Les Miserables* (1862). Before that he had written in exile a violent satire against Napoleon.

  rudoyer   to treat roughly.

  letter from Swinburne   EG had written to ACS for comments on his own verse, shortly before his 18th birthday. See *EG* p. 70.

p. 60   **July 10, 1868**   For various accounts of ACS's accident at the BM see *EG* pp. 71–2.

       Aubrey Beardsley   (1872–1898) often produced drawings that were disturbing and grotesque.

       Cupido crucifixus   The paradox of a crucified Cupid.

       "the kind hostess"   Mrs Ford Madox Brown.

p. 61   **"as Cowley said of Pindar"**   Abraham Cowley (1618–1667), English poet, of Pindar (522–443 BC), the greatest of the Greek lyric poets. "The phoenix Pindar is a vast species alone" in "In Praise of Pindar" from Cowley's *Pindaric Odes*. Compare EG's conclusion to the following portrait of Patmore.

       caricatures   notably by Max Beerbohm, including one of EG and ACS together.

       "lasso papavere collo demisere caput"   Virgil, Aeneid IX, 436: "as poppies with tired neck bow their heads".

p. 62   **"humble post"**   EG, aged 26 in 1875, was a Junior Assistant or Transcriber in the BM, now the British Library.

       "his own lodgings"   3 Great James Street.

p. 63   **"at home with us"**   29 Delamere Terrace.

       the baby   Tessa, EG's eldest child, was born on 14 September 1877, so was not quite four months old. Clara Watts-Dunton (*Home Life of Swinburne*, 1922) said ACS's "two pet subjects" were the sea and babies, but "people took care that he only saw their babies when on their best behaviour".

       George Eliot   (1819–1880), the distinguished author of *Middlemarch* etc.

       myrmidons   ACS presumably refers to G H Lewes and his journalist colleagues. The word, meaning unquestioning followers, comes from the Thessalian followers of Achilles at Troy.

p. 64   **"the devoted friend"**   Theodore Watts-Dunton. EG did not always think of him so charitably. He came to fear that Watts-Dunton had prejudiced ACS against him and to feel that ACS's sobriety had been at the cost of both his poetry and his essential character. In October 1909 EG wrote to T J Wise protesting at the idea that Watts-Dunton "should go down to posterity as the Hero-Friend". See *EG* p. 475.

p. 65   **Admiral Swinburne**   Charles Henry (1797–1877) always showed parental concern and responsibility for ACS. "We feel him to be safe while he is here", the Admiral wrote to Lord Houghton from Holmwood, 28 July 1867.

       "Thalassius"   a poem of idealized autobiography, not published until 1880.

       "Wasted Garden"   EG seems to be confusing two titles "A Wasted Vigil" and "A Forsaken Garden". The poem referred to must be the latter.

p. 66   **Ashburnham**   ACS's mother, Lady Jane, was the fourth daughter of the third Earl of Ashburnham.

       "Bothwell"   The contract with Chatto for "Bothwell" was dated April 1874.

       Edward Burne-Jones   (1833–1898), painter.

       Arthur O'Shaughnessy   (1844–1881), poet. See note p.146.

       P B Marston   (1850–1887), the blind poet, was O'Shaughnessy's brother-in-law.

       the Lizard   A peninsula in Cornwall famous for a local stone known as serpentine. ACS writes about it in "Tristram of Lyonesse".

       "I shall sleep . . . "   A stanza from "The Triumph of Time".

       publication of *Life*   It was much delayed; EG had begun work on it even before ACS's death in 1909. It was finally published in 1917. See *EG* pp. 474–81.

p. 67   **reviews**   Some were excellent. EG said of the one in the *Times Literary Supplement* "the truth is even better than the dreams". But the *New Statesman* reviewer and many others chided EG for heeding "the voice of that old Dame,

Discretion". And Ezra Pound attacked EG in *Poetry* (Chicago) and wrote of ACS "coated with a veneer of British officialdom and decked out for a psalm-singing audience".

p. 67   **"certain friends"**   included A C Benson and Maurice Baring, to whom EG wrote a clear exposition of the problems: "I ought to have been more daring, less reserved". See *EG* p. 480.

flagitious   evil. EG had first written simply 'worse'.

De Quincey   (1785–1859) admitted his own addiction in *Confessions of an English Opium-Eater* (1821).

p. 68   **heightened**   EG's typist and C Y Lang read this as 'brightened'.

Isabel Swinburne   ACS was the eldest of six children. His sister Isabel was initially friendly to EG when he wrote to her about his entry on ACS for DNB, but when it appeared two letters were published in the *Times* over her name attacking EG. The suggestion is the letters were written under the influence of **Mrs Disney Leith** (born Mary Gordon), a cousin who had been very close to ACS when they were young. It has been suggested she was the only woman ACS ever loved and the subject of "The Triumph of Time" and "Dolores". If this were true, it would account for her scorn for EG's identification of Adah Isaacs Menken with Dolores – the poem anyway written long before ACS met her. Jean Overton Fuller (*Swinburne* 1968) also suggested from evidence in the BM that Mary Leith shared ACS's interest in flagellation.

Lord Redesdale   1st Baron (1837–1916), diplomat, close friend of EG, grandfather of the Mitford sisters and a cousin of ACS and Mrs Leith.

Adah Isaacs Menken   (1835–1868) American actress. See note p.152.

p. 69   **Mr Wise**   T J Wise (1859–1937), whom EG never knew to be a forger. See *EG* pp. 390–4.

Lord Crewe   (1858–1945) was one of many peers with whom EG became very friendly during his years as Librarian of the House of Lords. Crewe was the son of Richard Monckton Milnes, Lord Houghton, who wrote the first biography of Keats and was a close friend of ACS. He was created Earl in 1895 and Marquess in 1911.

Lord Bryce   James Bryce (1838–1922), created Viscount in 1914.

Lord Sheffield   Edward Lyulph (1839–1925), 4th Baron Stanley of Alderley and 4th Baron Sheffield.

Richard Burton   (1821–1890), explorer and anthropologist, well known for his interest in sexual behaviour and deviance.

Lord Houghton   (1809–1885) see above.

p. 70   **"did not know he was a drunkard"**   William Morris used to tell a story on this theme. See *EG* pp. 114–5.

p. 71   **at Whistler's**   James Abbott McNeill Whistler (1834–1903), American painter.

Cameron   William Rossetti says in his diary that ACS had got to know Consul Cameron through Burton. Cameron died in 1870, not long after the incident at the Arts Club.

p. 72   **page 198 of *Life***   EG says: "in circumstances which were widely related at the time, he had a difference with the Committee . . . ".

W Bell Scott   (1811–1890), poet, painter, art critic, was closely associated with the Pre-Raphaelites. He decorated EG's poems *On Viol and Flute*, which were dedicated to him. EG met Scott as a result of a fan letter in 1870 and it was through him he came to know ACS.

Walter Pater   (1839–1894), a leading figure in the aesthetic movement, is sometimes credited with first using the phrase "art for art's sake".

p. 72   **Theodore Watts**   did not take the name Watts-Dunton until 1896. See above for note on him.

p. 73   **Titian**   (1477–1576) has given his name to a reddish-brown he often used for hair in his paintings.

Paris Bordone   (c.1500–1571), born at Treviso in Italy, was a painter of the Venetian school, a pupil of Titian.

Mathilde Blind   (1841–1896) There are a number of letters to her in C Y Lang's edition of ACS's letters. She was born in Germany with the name Cohen and came to London as a child in 1849.

kill Bismarck   The attempt on the life of the Prime Minister of Prussia (later first Chancellor of the German Reich) was in May 1866. Cohen committed suicide in prison.

Karl Blind   It was in the house of the German exile in London that ACS met his hero Mazzini, the Italian patriot, in March 1867. EG has a rather inaccurate account in his *Life of ACS*.

p. 74   *Justine*   The Marquis de Sade published this in 1791. Like his other books, it shows an obsessive interest in sexual pathology.

"Charenton"   published by James Pope-Hennessy in *Monckton Milnes's The Flight of Youth* (1951). Milnes's collection of erotic books included the first serious collection of de Sade.

near Dorset Square   ACS lived at 22a Dorset Square for three years from early summer 1865.

Savile Clarke   C Y Lang (see above) notes that Clarke was a "Bohemian and Fleet Streeter".

p. 75   **George R Sims**   His reminiscences *My Life: Sixty Years' Recollections of Bohemian London* (1917) are a source of information about Clarke and Thomson and the house of flagellation.

"mysterious house"   7 Circus Road, St John's Wood, in an area of London "which no Forsyte entered without open disapproval and secret curiosity", according to Galsworthy, *The Man of Property* (1906), Ch.7.

Adah Menken   described in 1888 in the Introduction to her poems (see below) as "the brilliant and beautiful woman who twenty-five years ago was the talk of two continents". Born in 1835, near New Orleans, she was put on the stage as a small child, but is said to have completed a translation of the Iliad at the age of twelve. She was certainly a good linguist and supported herself at one point by teaching French and Latin.

"Mazeppa"   As a page at the Polish court, Mazeppa was detected in an affair and the injured husband ordered him to be bound naked to the back of an untamed horse. There have been several versions of his story, including one by Byron and various burlesques. Menken was the first woman to attempt the part. *Mazeppa*, after its success in America, appeared at the Victoria Theatre in the Waterloo Road in London.

"married many times"   She had four husbands.

p. 76   **"Dolores her real name"**   That was not so; her baptismal name was Adelaide. ACS certainly called her Dolores (for example in a letter to Thomas Purnell, 9 December 1867). His poem "Dolores" had been published in *Poems and Ballads* (1866).

26th January   letter to ACS's Welsh friend, George Powell.

photograph   In a further letter to Powell (17 April 1968) ACS reports on "its publication and sale all over London".

p. 76   **to Paris**   She was rehearsing a play which was to open in early July, when she was taken ill. She is buried in Père Lachaise, the same cemetery as Oscar Wilde.
"her poetry"   A volume *Infelicia* was dedicated to Charles Dickens with his permission and published in 1867. It was reissued in 1888, with a biographical introduction.
poems on flagellation   The BM holds *The Whippingham Papers* and *The Flogging Block*, not in the General Catalogue. See Jean Overton Fuller, *Swinburne* p. 256.

p. 77   **some professional artist**   Simeon Solomon (1840–1905). Three pencil illustrations survive bound by T J Wise with *The Flogging Block* MS.
the letters   The BM holds a letter (MS Ashley 1755) from EG to Wise, suggesting that "the enclosed letters from Simeon Solomon" which "contain direct reference to his notorious vices and an implication that ACS was quite aware of their nature" should be destroyed. They were not and the nine letters are preserved at the BM together with some other letters – to Mary Leith in cypher – which EG also asked Wise to destroy.
Dorset Street   EG means Dorset Square, which is just north of Marylebone Road and a short walk from Regent's Park.
Songs before Sunrise   The volume was published in 1871.

COVENTRY PATMORE

p. 81   **Church of Rome**   CP joined the Church in 1864 when he was over 40. He met his second wife when in Rome undergoing instruction from a Jesuit.
Cardinal Manning   Henry Edward Manning (1808–1892), Roman Catholic Archbishop of Westminster in 1865, who left the Anglican Church in 1851. DNB refers to his "autocratic methods". Manning founded the Catholic temperance society, the League of the Cross.
"matters of philosophy"   Manning published a number of philosophical papers, including *Religio Viatoris* (1887), a statement of the philosophical basis of his own faith.
Basil Champneys   CP's friend, an architect, published a two-volume *Memoirs and Correspondence of CP* in 1900. He had access to all the papers but suppressed a good deal for the sake of the third and last Mrs Patmore.

p. 82   **Omar Khayyam's disdain**   See *Rubaiyat*, stanza 30 of Fitzgerald's second version: "Myself when young did eagerly frequent . . . " "All Poets and Prophets have hated priests as a class," CP wrote to EG in 1896, in a letter which compared Fitzgerald's translation with a prose one by Charles Pickering.
"his closest friend"   Basil Champneys. See above.
Schopenhauer   (1788–1860), known for his pessimistic philosophy embodied in *Die Welt als Wille und Vorstellung* (*The World as Will and Idea*, 1819). He thought God, free will and the immortality of the soul were all illusions.
Nietzsche   (1844–1900) EG's use of 1888 is not clear. The German philosopher's major book *Beyond Good and Evil* was published in England in 1886.

p. 83   **Archbishop Magee**   William Connor Magee (1821–1891), Archbishop of York in 1891, less than two months before his death. His remark that he would rather see England free than sober is quoted in *DNB*.
Herrick   Robert Herrick (1591–1674). ACS called him "the greatest song-writer ever born of English race".
Goethe   (1749–1832), the German writer, was immensely admired in Victorian

Britain, partly through the influence of Carlyle and George Eliot, who helped
G H Lewes with Goethe's biography.

p. 84 **Emperor William**   The German army defeated France at Worth on 6 August
1870, one of the crucial battles in the Franco-Prussian War. William of Hohenzol-
lern became Emperor of Germany at Versailles the following January, and Augusta
his Empress.

John Singer Sargent   (1856–1925), born in Florence of American parents, was
a close friend of EG. See *EG* pp. 265–7.

p. 85 **Hastings**   CP moved there in 1880 to "the Milward Mansion, a large ancient
house . . . in the centre of the old town". EG elsewhere recalls walking along the
Parade on a stormy night, "drenched by fountains of spray", with CP in ecstacy.

Pacha   or Pasha, a Turkish courtesy title, it suggests someone who regarded
women as totally inferior.

"a wilderness of fair women"   Compare Chaucer's "A Dream of Fair Women".

p. 86 **Tennyson**   failed to write to CP after his first wife's death and they never met
again, but Hallam Tennyson told Basil Champneys that his father often wondered
why CP had "given him up". Derek Patmore devotes a chapter of his biography
of CP (1949) to CP's friendship with AT, saying "a conspiracy of silence surrounds"
the subject. CP's second son was called Tennyson Patmore.

Emerson   Ralph Waldo Emerson (1803–1882) did much to further the reputation of CP's poetry in the United States.

Browning   RB wrote a poem about CP's first wife, Emily, called "A Face".

Rossetti, Millais, Woolner   Rossetti introduced CP's 1844 poems to the artists
John Millais (1829–1896) and Thomas Woolner (1825–1892). They were all closely
involved in the Pre-Raphaelite Brotherhood. CP was listed as one of the Immortals
in the manifesto drawn up by the Brotherhood. Millais painted a portrait of Emily
Patmore, now in the Fitzwilliam Museum, Cambridge. Woolner made medallion
portraits of both CP and his wife. Derek Patmore (see above) says that CP "kept
the friendship of Woolner . . . all his life", and, in 1875, he attempted to renew
the friendship with Rossetti.

to Lymington   CP had moved from Hastings to the Lodge on the estuary at
Lymington in 1891.

p. 87 **the Prophet Ezekiel,**   while captive in Babylon, foretold the destruction of Jerus-
alem and denounced the sins of the people.

Uzzah   See 2 Samuel 6:7, where the anger of the Lord is kindled by Uzzah
and "he died by the Ark of God". Obscure Biblical references such as this remind
the reader of EG's intensely Bible-centred upbringing.

Pandarus,   in medieval romance, is represented as a despicable pimp, though
there seems to be no classical basis for this. "Let all pitiful goers-between be
called to the world's end after my name." Shakespeare *Troilus and Cressida* Act
3, Sc.2.

Ruskin   John Ruskin (1819–1900) was also an admirer of Emily Patmore. It
was CP who persuaded Ruskin to write his famous letter to the *Times* in 1851,
defending the Pre-Raphaelites.

Archilochus   a celebrated Greek poet, probably of the seventh century BC.
Eustathius spoke of him as "scorpion-tongued".

"The Toys"   is probably CP's best-known poem: the father regrets his harshness
to his son.

"If I were Dead"   also contains regret. It begins with a quotation from one of
CP's children: "If I were dead, you'd sometimes say, Poor Child!"

p. 88 **the Phoenix**   was said to live for 500 (or 1000) years, burn itself to ashes and

154

rise renewed from the flames. "There never was but one Phoenix." (*Brewer's Readers' Handbook*).

WALT WHITMAN

p. 90   **"several accounts"**   WW's English visitors included Robert Buchanan (*A Look Round Literature*, 1887), Sir Edwin Arnold (*Seas and Lands*, 1891) and Oscar Wilde (interview in the *Century*, November 1882).

"unwilling to go"   It is just possible EG had forgotten his own passionate discipleship as a young man. His admiring letter to WW (12 December 1873), written after reading *Leaves of Grass*, survives. See *With Walt Whitman in Camden*, Horace Traubel, Boston, 1906, p. 245. Traubel to WW: "'I call that pretty good.' 'So do I,' said he. 'Gosse must have been young then. Does he last?' W smiled, 'Who knows? . . . I am used to defections – especially of the young enthusiasts that grow old – yes, old and cold.'" See also William White in *Victorian Studies*, 1, ii (December 1957).

p. 91   **"in Boston"**   EG was actually in New York, not as far away as he suggests.

"received a note"   In fact, EG had written himself to WW on 29 December 1884. Traubel (*With Walt Whitman*) quotes Whitman as saying: "I have a letter here somewhere in which Gosse announced that he would come." The note EG mentions was in reply. See *EG* p. 257. EG's memory was notoriously inaccurate, but certainly he wanted to give the impression both at the time and, later, in this 1893 essay, that the approach came from Whitman.

2nd January 1885   EG made good use of his night in Philadelphia, sharing a box with General Sherman at a performance of Browning's *A Blot in the 'Scutcheon*. See *EG* p. 258.

328 Mickle Street   WW had bought the house in March 1884 and was apparently happy with it but EG was not alone in thinking it a dreary place. In his diary written at the time EG calls it simply "modest".

"a melancholy woman"   Mrs Mary Davis, WW's housekeeper.

"nice old gentleman"   WW was then only 64 – but 30 years older than Gosse.

"Is that my friend?"   In EG's diary: "Genial manner. 'My friend.'"

"his own dwelling-room"   A photo in *Walt Whitman: a study* by John Addington Symonds (1893) shows more chairs but otherwise fits closely with EG's description, including the spotted wallpaper and "mountains of paper in wild confusion". From these, as Traubel (*With Walt Whitman*) describes, WW would from time to time extract exactly what he wanted.

p. 92   **'hodden'**   was a coarse woollen cloth made by rural weavers on their hand-looms. Grey hodden was made without dyeing, from a mixture of fleeces. It is seen, according to *SOED*, as "typical of rusticity".

shirt, wide open   R M Bucke in *Walt Whitman* (Philadelphia, 1883) confirms EG's description. "The only thing peculiar about his dress was that he had no necktie at any time" and always wore shirts that exposed the throat and "upper part of the breast". "Everything he wore, and everything about him, was always scrupulously clean."

"like a cat"   From EG, a cat-lover, this was high praise.

p. 93   **Issachar**   was one of the twelve sons of Jacob. "Issachar is a strong ass couching down between two burdens", Genesis 49:14.

Valmiki   was the reputed author of the *Ramayana*, one of the two great epics of India. It had been translated into English in Benares by R T H Griffiths in five volumes, 1870–74.

p. 93 **Catlin** George Catlin (1796–1872) devoted his life to the North American Indian. Between 1829 and 1838 he painted 600 Indian portraits.

Starting from Paumanok (1860) was included in the third edition of *Leaves of Grass*. It was originally called "Proto-Leaf".

"one of his greatest friends" In the diary entry Gosse appears to have written "Portrait of Harlan", but he must have been inaccurate in recording the name. WW often talked of Harlan but this was not the handsome oarsman, but James Harlan, Secretary of the Interior, who had dismissed Whitman from his job "as a clerk in the Interior Office" after reading *Leaves of Grass*. It is possible the portrait was of Thomas Harned, who was a close friend of WW. Edwin Haviland Miller, editor of WW's *Correspondence*, 1964, suggests the picture was of WW's young Canadian friend, Tom Nicholson.

p. 94 **"yawp"** to utter a strident call, to yelp as a dog. WW had used the phrase "sound my barbaric yawp" in the final section of "Song of Myself". EG had echoed this in a verse for John Blaikie in October 1869: "One Western maniac 'yawps' a turbid song" (see *EG* p. 82), which suggests EG's first feelings about WW were not as enthusiastic as those in his 1873 letter. In 1907 EG reviewed a book by Bliss Perry on WW and wrote to Perry. (See *Life and Letters of Sir Edmund Gosse* by Evan Charteris, 1931). "The real psychology of W.W. would be enormously interesting. I think the keynote would be a staggering ignorance, a perhaps wilful non-perception of the real physical conditions of his nature."

"a preface to some new edition" WW was perhaps already working on the "Note at Beginning" and "Note at End" for the 1888 *Complete Poems and Prose* or even "A Backward Glance O'er Travel'd Roads", though this did not appear until the 1889 edition of *Leaves of Grass*.

"a dim impression" One thing EG had apparently forgotten, or preferred not to remember, was that he had shared his visit to Whitman with, as his diary records, "Miss Smith and her friend, Boston enthusiasts." Miss Smith was Mary, Logan Pearsall Smith's sister, who had been in EG's audience for his Boston lectures. (See *EG* p. 257.)

Shelley in his "Stanzas written in Dejection, near Naples" 111.2:

> Alas! I have nor hope nor health,
> Nor peace within nor calm around,
> Nor that content surpassing wealth
> The sage in meditation found,
> And walked with inward glory crowned –

WOLCOTT BALESTIER

p. 96 **Mrs Humphry Ward** Mary Augusta Ward (1851–1920), novelist and social worker, was a grand-daughter of Dr Arnold of Rugby and a niece of Matthew Arnold. At this time she had just published her novel *Robert Elsmere* (1888), which became a best-seller.

Henry James On 6 June 1890 James sent to his sister an "admirable" letter from Balestier and wrote, "I send the letter mainly to illustrate the capital intelligence and competence of Balestier and show you in what good hands I am. He will probably strike you, as he strikes me, as the perfection of an 'agent'." *Letters of Henry James* ed. Lubbock (1920) vol.1, p. 170.

p. 96 **atonic**   unharmonious
W D Howells   (1837–1920) was one of America's leading men of letters. He was extremely influential through his contributions to the *Atlantic Monthly* – which he edited from 1871 to 1881 – and *Harper's*. At this point he was more successful as a novelist than James. He and EG had become friends in 1882. See *EG* pp. 244–5.

p. 97 ***Benefits Forgot***   was finished in 1890.
"a New York publisher"   John W Lovell.
George Meredith and Mr Thomas Hardy   Meredith had died by the time the essay was published so does not get an honorific. Balestier's relations with neither of them seem to have been close. Hardy wrote to his wife on 9 December 1890: "Balestier pursues me with telegrams –" *Collected Letters* ed. Purdy and Millgate vol.1, 1978, p. 223.

p. 98 ***John Inglesant***   J H Shorthouse (1834–1903) published this historical novel in 1880. EG used to stay with him when he lectured in Birmingham.

p. 99 **"a new Indian writer"**   *Soldiers Three*, a collection of stories, was first published by the Pioneer Press in Allahabad in 1888 and not in England until 1890. RK left India on 3 March 1889, arriving in London in October that year, just at the time EG was mentioning him to Balestier.
"future collaborator"   Balestier and RK wrote *The Naulahka* together, Balestier the American scenes, RK the Indian. It was first published in the *Century*, starting in November 1891, through EG's negotiation, just before Balestier's death. Lord Birkenhead, in his biography of RK wrote, "Reading the dry, stilted chapters contributed by Balestier about life in the Middle West, one is again astonished by the spell that this man exercised."

p. 100 **"Mr Norris"**   W E Norris (1847–1925), novelist. Henry James's Christmas letters to him (Yale) regularly contained an assessment of EG, their mutual friend.
novels   *The Oxford Companion to English Literature* picks out *A Fair Device* for mention and gives its date as 1886.

p. 101 **"became his brother-in-law"**   RK married Caroline Balestier on 18 January 1892, five weeks after her brother's funeral. "Henry James gave away the bride and I supported the bridegroom," EG wrote in a letter. See *EG* p. 332. RK's biographers say Ambrose Poynter was RK's best man.
"for business reasons"   These concerned the English Library, a new soft-cover publishing imprint Balestier and Heinemann were setting up to challenge Tauchnitz on the continent.
"For what was he? Some novel power . . . "   From Tennyson's "In Memoriam" CXII, lines 9–12. EG has changed "thee" to "him" in the final line.

THOMAS HARDY

p. 103 **"at Princeton"**   This item is published with permission from Princeton University and Jennifer Gosse.

p. 104 **"rather inaccurate"**   "ennui" was rendered as "Anouilh" and "passion" as "fashion", for instance.
Arthur Benson   (1862–1925) and EG were staying at the Digby Hotel, Sherborne, in September 1912, the last holiday they took together. For their relationship, see *EG*, particularly pp. 371–6, 426–7, 442–9. (In those last pages I quote

from Benson's diary his version of this visit.) See also David Newsome *On the Edge of Paradise* (1980) pp. 283–4. Benson at this time was a Fellow of Magdalene College, Cambridge; he became Master in 1915. TH became an Honorary Fellow of Magdalene in November 1913.

p. 104 **"reddened our faces"**   Motoring in 1912 exposed one to the elements. Henry James once said how beneficial motoring was to his health, something no-one today would suggest.

Wessex   TH had first used the name Wessex for his fictional region in *Far from the Madding Crowd* (1874). In a letter in about 1888, he wrote "I find that the name Wessex, wh. I was the first to use in fiction, is getting to be taken up everywhere." See *The Collected Letters of Thomas Hardy* vol.1 (1978) ed. Purdy and Millgate, p. 171. By 1912 it was firmly established as a term for Dorset and adjoining areas of south-western England.

"stunted"   was a second thought for "small". TH was five feet six inches, five inches shorter than EG.

"yeoman"   was a second thought for "peasant". In his diary, Benson had written that TH's was the face, not of a farmer or peasant, "but of a village tradesman". At Max Gate, he saw him as looking like "a retired half-pay officer from a not very smart regiment". Others saw him differently. J M Barrie to Cynthia Asquith on 6 June 1920: "There is something about him more attractive than I find in almost any other man – a simplicity that really merits the adjective *divine* – I could see some of the disciples having been thus." *Letters of J M Barrie*, ed. V Meynell (1942).

"autochthonous"   is explained in the next phrase. Autochthons are the original inhabitants of a place.

"the Chalk Man",   otherwise known as the Cerne Giant, is nearly 200 feet in length. Hermann Lea in *Thomas Hardy's Wessex* (1913) says that at that time, far from thinking Caesar might have seen him, "by most antiquarians it is thought to represent the work of medieval monks from the abbey below". But he adds that probably its origin is in a more remote past, and certainly there is nothing Christian in its phallic challenge, as EG suggests. It has also been thought to be Hercules.

"dapper"   was a second thought for "modern".

Max Gate   Hardy's house, designed by him and built by his father and brother in 1884/5, lies just to the south-east of Dorchester, off the Wareham road. Now, in the late 20th century, it is on the very edge of the bypass, but fortunately still surrounded by trees, though few remain of the immense Scots pines that were there in 1912.

"twenty-five years ago"   EG had first stayed there in August 1886.

"pale"   orginally "poor" and then "soft".

p. 105 **"the little house"**   Benson thought it both mean and pretentious and considered it "airless and dark, like a house wrapped up and put away in a box". Diary quoted by Newsome, op.cit.

Emma Hardy   Benson describes "the crazy and fantastic wife" and mentions the presence of her niece, Lilian Gifford, ignored by EG in his account. Emma died only two months after this visit.

"some nymph"   Michael Millgate in *Thomas Hardy: A Biography* (1982) writes of Emma that summer "dressed in her usual girlish outfit of white frock and blue sash".

"he talked"   but Benson recorded that TH seemed to display "the suspiciousness of the rustic, the idea that he must guard himself, not give himself away".

croquet-ground   Lilian Gifford, according to Benson, wanted to play croquet but was thwarted.

p. 106   **"experience"**   EG first wrote "life".

Desperate Remedies   published in 1871. Millgate (op.cit.), p. 117, says "Hardy now acted all too literally upon the advice he had received from George Meredith and made of *Desperate Remedies* a heavily plotted and deliberately sensational work." Meredith was then working for Chapman and Hall and his advice followed his reading of "the first book of all", *The Poor Man and the Lady*, which Macmillan had already turned down.

"tore it all up"   but not before he had drawn on it for later books – including the novella *An Indiscretion in the Life of an Heiress* and *Desperate Remedies* itself.

"knew so much about women"   See Millgate, *Thomas Hardy* pp. 119, 84–5 etc.

p. 107   **"a solemn occasion"**   Dr Johnson's funeral was in Westminster Abbey on 20 December 1784. William Gerard Hamilton (1729–96) held several administrative posts in the government of his day.

"fifty-three years"   It seems that EG and TH first met at a Savile Club dinner in the winter of 1874. See EG: *Silhouettes* (1925): "The Savile Club".

"grossly and fanatically attacked"   There were violent reactions to both *Tess of the d'Urbervilles* and *Jude the Obscure*. See Millgate *Thomas Hardy* pp. 319–21, 368–74.

concinnity   harmony, congruity.

p. 108   **"over-estimate his poetry"**   TH certainly at the end of his life put most value on his poems. That he rated himself very highly as a poet is perhaps indicated by his pointing out to Macmillan that if there were any problem about the length of his *Selected Poems*, which he was revising just before his death, the corresponding Wordsworth volume contained an even greater number. See Millgate *Thomas Hardy* p. 565. It was prescient of EG to realize that in time Hardy's poetry and novels would be equally valued.

"pessimism"   TH constantly denied the description of himself as "pessimistic", a word, he said, "beloved of the paragraph gents". See letter to Middleton Murry, 9 December 1920, Purdy and Millgate *Collected Letters* vol.6 (1987) p. 51. Eleven days later TH despairingly quoted one reviewer who had said: "Truly this pessimism is insupportable . . . One marvels that Hardy is not in a madhouse." On 7 November 1905 (vol.3, 1982) p. 187, TH had written to EG, "Why people make the mistake of supposing pessimists, or what are called such, incurably melancholy, I do not know. The very fact of their having touched bottom gives them a substantial cheerfulness in the consciousness that they have nothing to lose."

"uneventful to the last degree"   TH was not so much of a recluse as EG suggests here. See Millgate, *Thomas Hardy*.

"sympathetic attention'   Clive Holland in *Thomas Hardy* (1933) records that he heard a mutual friend of the Hardys, after TH's death, say that he owed ten years of his life to his second wife's care and attention. He had married Florence Dugdale in 1914.

"If this be she . . . "   EG has adapted stanza XXXV of Shelley's *Adonais*.

LADY DOROTHY NEVILL

p. 109   **Lady Burghclere**   (1869–1933), daughter of 4th Earl of Carnarvon, married first Captain Hon. Alfred Byng, son of 2nd Earl of Strafford and, after his death, in 1890 Herbert Gardner, Lord Burghclere, Liberal member of Parliament, President of the Board of Agriculture and translator of the Georgics into English verse. At 48 Charles Street, the Burghcleres had been neighbours of DN. Lady Burghclere herself published lives of George Villiers, 2nd Duke of Buckingham and of James, 1st Duke of Ormonde.

p. 109   **"the death of our friend"**   DN died 24 March 1913.

"three thick volumes"   In fact, there appear to have been five: *Recollections* 1906; *Leaves from the Notebooks of Lady Dorothy Nevill* 1907; *More Leaves* 1908, *Under Five Reigns* 1910 and *My Own Times* 1912.

"all these months"   nine months or so. The essay is dated January 1914.

p. 110   **Mr Ralph Nevill**   (1865–1930) 3rd son of DN, who served in the Foreign Office and Admiralty and published a number of books. His entry in *Who's Who* credits him with editing his mother's reminiscences.

Sir Redvers and Lady Audrey Buller   General Rt. Hon. Sir Redvers Buller (1839–1908) married Lady Audrey, daughter of the 4th Marquis Townshend in 1882. Buller won the VC in the Zulu War, 1879; later he was Chief of Staff in Sudan and led the relief of Ladysmith in the Boer War. For EG's friendship with them, see *EG* pp. 363, 402 etc. At one point, EG called Lady Audrey "my faithful familiar".

Thomas Bell   (1792–1880) wrote the reptile section of Darwin's *Zoology of the Voyage of the Beagle* and was President of the Linnean Society and FRS. He was a cousin of EG's father, son of his aunt Susan, who was herself a naturalist.

"my father"   P H Gosse (1810–1888) was primarily a marine biologist but had written on entomology, for instance in an 1848 paper "on the insects of Jamaica".

Watts' picture   G F Watts (1817–1904) painted her at the Palazzo S. Clemente in Florence in about 1845. DN herself regarded it as an "idealized study".

p. 111   **"her children"**   three sons and one daughter.

p. 112   **Madame du Deffand**   (1697–1780) was one of the most celebrated French women of her time. She corresponded with Walpole and Voltaire.

D.V.   *Deo volente*, God willing.

"old Lord Wharncliffe"   1st Earl of and 3rd Baron (1827–1899). His London house was in Curzon Street, Mayfair. He owned "about 33,000 acres of Yorkshire".

Mr George Russell   (1853–1919) grandson of 6th Duke of Bedford, Liberal MP, Under-Secretary of State for India, 1892–4 and writer of a number of books.

p. 113   **Elizabeth Fry**   (1780–1845) and **Florence Nightingale** (1820–1910) were both pioneer reformers, the one of prisons, the other of the nursing profession.

guignols   Guignol was the French "Punch", the leading character in a popular puppet show. The word came to mean any sort of show. Grand Guignol was a theatre in Paris that specialized in horror plays, but little guignols presumably had nothing to do with horror.

p. 114   **boutades**   brusque sallies.

Charles Street   her house at 45, just off Berkeley Square, was in the heart of Mayfair.

Eridge Castle   in Sussex was her husband's childhood home. He was heir until the birth of his cousin, 3rd Earl of Abergavenny. The "quadrupeds" included deer; the deerpark, according to DN, was probably the only one in England to survive as it had been at the Norman Conquest.

"which is the bliss of solitude"   Wordsworth's much quoted lines from "The Daffodils" actually refer to "the inward eye" not ear.

p. 115   **"old Horace Walpole's talent"**   DN was happy to claim the great Walpole

(1717–1797) as her "kinsman". "His literary reputation rests largely on his letters", according to the current *Oxford Companion to English Literature*.

p. 115 **"a fantastic variety of strangely coloured paper"** Victorian etiquette books allowed such indulgence, which would today be thought vulgar.

p. 116 **Mr John Burns** (1858–1943) was a Radical MP, 1892–1918 and President of the Local Government Board 1905–1914.

"Mr Birhell" Augustine Birrell (1850–1933), second husband of the widow of Tennyson's son, Lionel, was at this time Chief Secretary for Ireland. He was a prolific writer.

Lord Wolseley (1833–1913) 1st Viscount. Commanded British troops in the Ashanti Wars, an expeditionary force to Egypt, the Gordon Relief Expedition and was later in Ireland.

the FM Field-Marshal, created 1894.

our CC Commander-in-Chief of the Army, 1895–1900.

at the House of Lords EG was Librarian from 1904 to 1914.

conventicle the word suggests a clandestine religious meeting.

Lord Lansdowne (1845–1927) 5th Marquess of Lansdowne. Lansdowne House was in Brook Street which backs on to Charles Street. Lansdowne had a country seat at Bowood Park, Calne, Wiltshire. He had a distinguished career in public service, including Governor-General of Canada and India, Secretary of State for War and Foreign Secretary.

p. 117 **the Human Elephant** Joseph Merrick, otherwise known as the Elephant Man, was treated by Frederick Treves, a good friend of EG, at the London Hospital (see later in the letter). He was recently the subject of a film starring John Hurt. EG writes interestingly about Merrick in his review of Treves's memoirs, reprinted in *Silhouettes* (1925). DN was one of three women Merrick thanked for having been very kind to him, in a note following a report in the Pathological Society's Transactions Vol.XXXVI, 1885.

p. 118 **Zola's Rougon-Macquart novels** appeared between 1871 and 1893: and included *L'Assommoir* in 1877, *La Terre* in 1887, and *La Bête Humaine* in 1890.

Endymion by Benjamin Disraeli appeared in 1880. It was his last completed novel.

Swinburne's death was in 1909.

Verlaine for EG's relations with Verlaine and his visit to England, see *EG* p. 370–1. The visit was actually in November 1893, not in 1894.

p. 119 **"grain of mustard-seed"** See Matthew 13:31 – "the least of all seeds: but when it is grown, it . . . becometh a tree."

the London Hospital in the Mile End Road in London's East End. It was here she became acquainted with the Elephant Man.

p. 120 **Koh-i-Noor** literally "mountain of light", was the name given to what was reputedly one of the most valuable diamonds in the world. It was presented to Queen Victoria in 1849.

Lady Airlie (1866–1956), widow of the 8th Earl, she was Lady Mabell, daughter of the 5th Earl of Arran. After DN's death, Lady Airlie became a particularly close friend of EG. In 1920 he received 90 letters, cards and notes from her.

dearest Winifred Lady Burghclere herself, to whom EG's open letter was addressed. See earlier note.

HENRY JAMES

p. 121 **"fruitful year"** 1876. HJ left Paris for London on 10 December.
Roderick Hudson had been published in Boston on 20 November 1875.
The American The serial began in the *Atlantic* in June 1876.

p. 122 **Daudet** Alphonse (1840–1897), French novelist.
Maupassant Guy de (1850–1893), French short story writer and novelist. Both can be called "naturalistic" writers, their styles simple and direct.
English society Six years later, still living in Bolton Street, off Piccadilly, HJ wrote in his journal: "I came to London as a complete stranger, and today I know much too many people. J'y suis absolument comme chez moi."
Greville Charles (1794–1865) kept a detailed diary from 1820 to 1860. HJ reviewed the first volume in 1875.
Crabb Robinson (1775–1867). His diaries provide valuable information about his friends who included Wordsworth, Coleridge and Hazlitt.

p. 123 **"some dinner party"** Their first meeting was almost certainly in the late summer of 1879 at a lunch party at the Savile with Andrew Lang and Robert Louis Stevenson. HJ's first visit to EG's home was in December 1882.
Hawthorne HJ's book preceded EG's *Gray* in John Morley's English Men of Letters series.
Mr (now Lord) Morley would later be opposed to HJ's award of the OM. See Edel, *Life of HJ* vol.2, section 118.
"an article on the drawings" HJ's article appeared in the *Century* in May 1883. EG was then the London agent of the *Century*.
George Du Maurier (1834–1896), artist and author of *Trilby* and a friend of EG.
"weakness of his spine" Edel considers HJ's back and quotes a letter to Howard Sturgis: "If you have a Back, for heaven's sake take care of it . . . I did bad damage . . . to mine, the consequence of which is that, in spite of the retarded attention, and years, really, of recumbency, later, I've been saddled with it for life."
"his mother having died" Mary James died 29 January 1882.

p. 124 **"illness of his father"** Henry James senior died 18 December 1882.
"wrote from Boston" the letter (2 April 1883) praising EG's *On Viol and Flute* is in *Selected Letters of HJ to EG* ed. Rayburn S Moore (Louisiana, 1988) p. 28. The letter suggests they were already on warm terms.
Colonel Higginson Thomas Wentworth (1823–1911), a remarkable man in his day (radical Unitarian minister, revolutionary Abolitionist, soldier, friend of Emerson) is now best remembered as Emily Dickinson's literary mentor.
Percy Lubbock (1879–1965), critic and biographer. His selection of HJ's letters was published in 1920.

p. 125 *The Bostonians* is now among the best known of HJ's novels. The letter EG refers to was of 25 August 1915. The novel's omission from the New York Edition (1907–1909) was originally "provisional". HJ wrote, "We always meant that that work shld. eventually come in. Revision of it loomed peculiarly formidable . . . " See Moore *Selected Letters* p. 314.
"an eminent author" John Addington Symonds. See *EG* pp. 247–248.

p. 126 *The Tragic Muse* published in 1890.

p. 127 **Daudet** See above.
Edmond de Goncourt (1822–1896) one of the two Goncourt brothers who wrote in close collaboration, kept a famous journal and gave their name to the Prix

Goncourt. Like Daudet, they were exponents of "Naturalism". Jules, the younger brother, had died in 1870.

p. 127 **the Daniel Curtises**   In a letter to EG in Italy in 1901 HJ called Daniel and Ariana (he a rich American expatriate, she the daughter of an English admiral) "the rare and racy Curtises". Their Palazzo was on the Grand Canal and is commemorated in *The Wings of the Dove*.

Edward Compton   (1854–1918) actor-manager, father of Compton Mackenzie and the actress Fay Compton.

"the strain, the anxiety . . . "   HJ to EG on 2 November 1891. It was a time of great anxiety for HJ – his sister Alice was dying. At one point, he wrote of her and his play as his two "invalids". Before Alice's death in March 1892, HJ suffered the death of his friend Wolcott Balestier. (See p. 101.)

Tenants   first called *Mrs Vibert*.

Disengaged   eventually called *Mrs Jasper's Way*. No-one wanted to produce either play under either title, though the latter got as far as having scenery under construction and costumes ordered.

p. 128 *The Album* and *The Reprobate* were both published in *Theatricals: Second Series* (NY, 1894).

"sordid developments"   HJ wrote at length about these to William James and his wife on 29 December 1893.

George Alexander   (1858–1918) actor-manager.

"I mean to wage this war"   Also from the letter cited above, 29 December 1893.

"never been printed"   *Guy Domville*, privately printed in 1894 to protect copyright, appeared in book form first in *The Complete Plays of Henry James*, 1949.

first night of *Guy Domville*   For a fuller description see *EG* pp. 379–80. EG is inaccurate in various particulars. He was a lunch guest the following day.

p. 130 **"roving for miles and miles"**   The area is flat and marshy, much of it land reclaimed from the sea. Winchelsea is south of Rye and the Romneys four times as far to the north-east, across Walland Marsh. New Romney is the largest town in the area and one of the ancient Cinque Ports; Old Romney, two miles to the west, is a very small village with a 14th-century chapel.

buisson d'épines   prickly; literally (botanically) it refers to the pyracantha.

"the desolate ghost of Dunwich"   Part of the small Suffolk town lies under the encroaching sea. HJ wrote to EG, 11 August 1897: "I toy with the dead men's bones . . . I quite adore the little place".

p. 131 **"a letter of September 25th"**   is to Arthur Benson and is in Lubbock's selection, which EG seems to have had on his desk while writing this essay. EG altered the letter, apparently to make it seem as if written to him himself. In the original "for 21 years" is followed not by "It was built about 1705" but by "One would think I was your age!" Benson was nearly 20 years younger than HJ, whereas EG was only six years younger. The length of the lease proved to be irrelevant as the owner died before long and HJ was able to buy the freehold.

"the Vivian of the stage"   Vivian was the dangerous seducer at Arthur's court who enchanted Merlin himself.

"a wonderful summer"   On 19 October 1898 HJ described to Frances Morse "this wonderful, hot, rainless, radiant summer."

p. 132 **"related by Archbishop Benson"**   Arthur Benson took HJ to stay with his family at Addington, the Archbishop of Canterbury's Palace near Croydon. There "a vague fragment of a tale he ineffectually tried to tell me" (as HJ wrote to EG, 12 October 1898) gave HJ the germ of *The Turn of the Screw*.

163

p. 132 **Lubbock . . . has described** in his preface to the Rye section of his edition of the Letters.

p. 134 **sacerdotal** as of a priest.

of the Français that is, of the Comédie Française, the French national theatre.

Jean-Baptiste Henri Lacordaire (1802–1861), French preacher and theologian who went into exile under Napoleon III. He was closely associated with

Sainte-Beuve Charles-Augustin (1804–1869), French literary critic. When EG received an honorary degree at the Sorbonne, he was described as "le Sainte-Beuve de l'outre manche".

p. 136 **Mrs Wharton** Edith (1862–1937), American novelist.

Valley of Decision published that year, 1902.

Guy de Maupassant See above.

the House of Lords EG had become Librarian in 1904.

p. 137 **definitive edition** known as the New York edition, published from 1907 to 1909.

the garden-room no longer exists. It was destroyed in 1940.

p. 138 **"in Cheyne Walk"** 21 Carlyle Mansions.

Mr Sargent John Singer Sargent (1856–1925), American painter, well known to both HJ and EG. HJ called the portrait "Sargent at his best and poor old HJ not at his worst; in short, a living breathing likeness and a masterpiece of painting." (HJ to Rhoda Broughton, 25 June 1913.)

"surprisingly mutilated" In May 1914 Mary Wood attacked the picture with a meat cleaver, wishing to demonstrate that nothing was safe "until women are given their political freedom."

"impaired by the tomahawk . . . doubly damaged" HJ, 6 May 1914, to Mrs Humphry Ward who was herself opposed to universal suffrage, on the grounds that women's influence could best be wielded in the home.

p. 139 **"the huge horror of blackness" etc** HJ wrote to Howard Sturgis, 4 August 1914: "How can what is going on not be to one as a huge horror of blackness? . . . The plunge of civilization into this abyss . . . " etc.

Roland Charlemagne's nephew, whose horn (oliphant) made the whole Saracen army fall back in terror. The defile of Roncesvalles was traditionally the scene of his death.

"shirked any one of the implications" HJ to his nephew Henry James junior, 6 August 1914, "For myself, I draw a long breath that we are not to have failed France or shirked any shadow of a single one of the *implications* of the Entente."

"bracing himself unutterably" HJ to Mrs W K Clifford, 31 August 1914, "bracing myself unutterably" etc.

Reims The Germans took Reims on 5 September 1914.

p. 140 **"sad fate of Belgium"** Belgium came under the control of the German army on 3 December 1914.

The Ivory Tower was to have been written in ten books, each section devoted to a different character. It was never completed, but published after HJ's death.

The Sense of the Past "The story of an American walking into a remote time" (Edel).

The Middle Years The fragment was published in 1917. It was also left incomplete and published posthumously. It is also the name of one of HJ's short stories and of one of Edel's volumes of biography.

p. 141 **"hesitations of Mr Wilson"** that is about bringing America into the war.

"he had a stroke" There was a second stroke on the following day which left HJ further paralysed and confused.

164

p. 141 **The Order of Merit** The only novelists previously admitted to the Order were Meredith and Hardy.
Lord Bryce James, Viscount (1838–1922), much involved at this point with promoting a League of Nations. *DNB* indicates no reason why he should have been deputed to deliver the OM.
"cremated" HJ's ashes were buried beside the graves of his mother and sister in Massachusetts.

Index to Names and Titles